Egypt

SIMON & SCHUSTER BOOKS FOR YOUNG READERS
An imprint of Simon & Schuster Children's Publishing Division
1230 Avenue of the Americas, New York, New York 10020

Conceived and produced by Weldon Owen Pty Ltd
61 Victoria Street, McMahons Point
Sydney, NSW 2060, Australia

Group Chief Executive Officer John Owen
President and Chief Executive Officer Terry Newell
Publisher Sheena Coupe
Creative Director Sue Burk
Concept Development John Bull, The Book Design Company
Editorial Coordinator Mike Crowton
Vice President, International Sales Stuart Laurence
Vice President, Sales and New Business Development Amy Kaneko
Vice President, Sales: Asia and Latin America Dawn Low
Administrator, International Sales Kristine Ravn

Project Editor Jennifer Losco
Designer John Bull, The Book Design Company
Cover Designers Gaye Allen and Kelly Booth

Color reproduction by Chroma Graphics (Overseas) Pte Ltd
Printed by SNP Leefung Printers Ltd
Manufactured in China

A WELDON OWEN PRODUCTION

SIMON & SCHUSTER BOOKS FOR YOUNG READERS is a trademark of Simon & Schuster, Inc.
The text for this book is set in Meta and Rotis Serif.
10 9 8 7 6 5 4 3 2
Cataloging-in-publication data for this book is available from the Library of Congress.

ISBN-13: 978-1-4169-3858-3
ISBN-10: 1-4169-3858-3

Egypt

Joyce Tyldesley

Simon & Schuster Books for Young Readers
New York London Toronto Sydney

Contents

Pyramids and Other Tombs

Temples and Towns

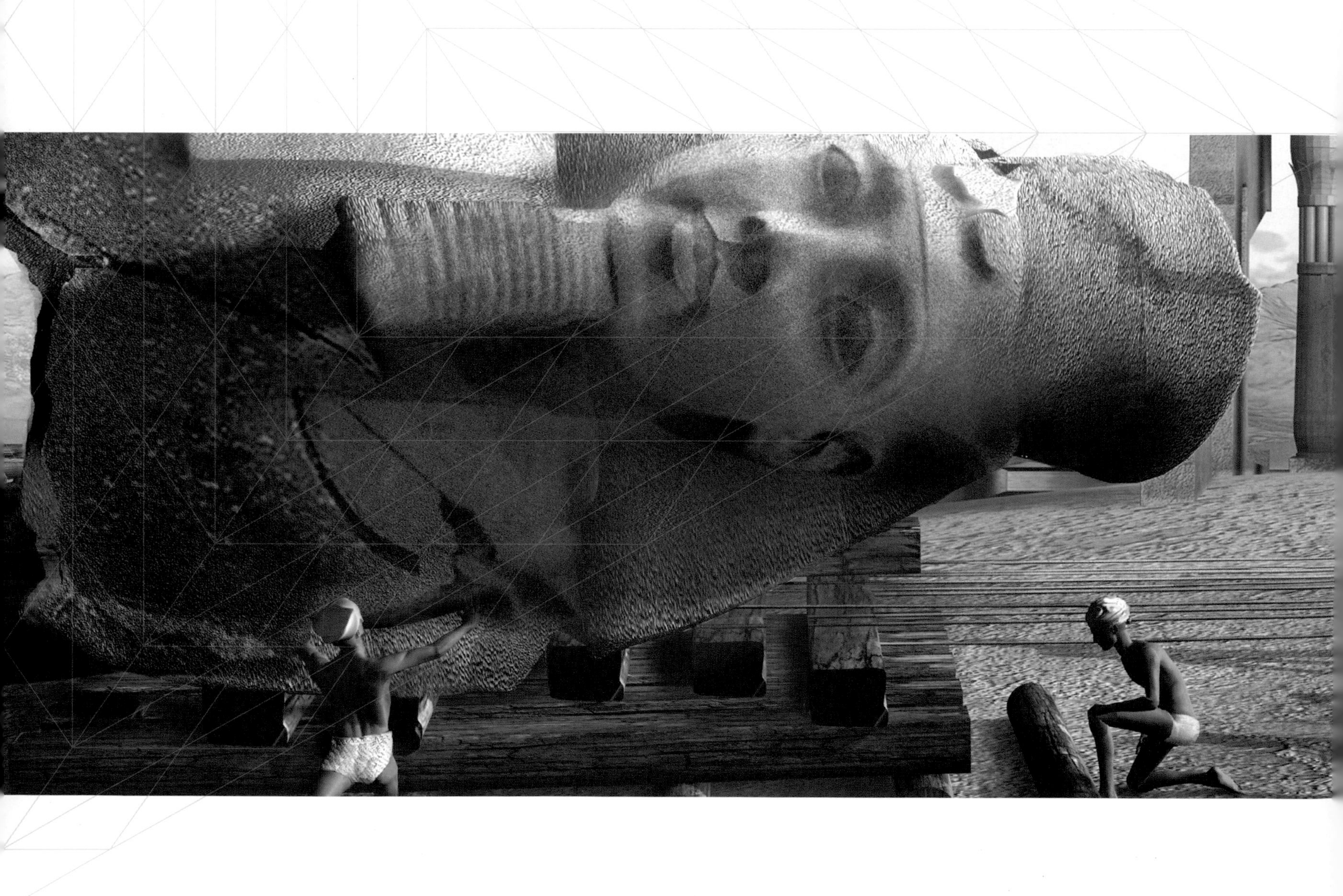

troducing

The Gift of
The Nile

The Greek historian Herodotus wrote that "Egypt is the gift of the Nile." He was right. Without the Nile, Egypt could not have survived. The Nile brought water, fish, and soil to Egypt. It served as both the main highway and the sewerage system. The fertile land that borders the Nile was known as the Black Land. Here the Egyptians grew crops and built mud-brick houses. The sterile desert land away from the Nile was known as the Red Land. Here the Egyptians built tombs and cemeteries.

Water for a dry land

The Nile flows northward through Egypt's Nile Valley (known as Upper, or Southern, Egypt) bringing much-needed water to a dry land. At Memphis, near modern Cairo, the river splits into several branches (the Nile Delta; known as Lower, or Northern, Egypt) before emptying into the Mediterranean Sea.

Nile River

Palestine, Syria, Israel, and Lebanon

Sinai

Gulf of Sue

Tanis

Mendes

Avaris and Per Ramesses

Bubastis

Cairo

Giza

Saqqara

Memphis

Dahshur

The Meidum cemetery includes a collapsed pyramid built by King Snefru.

Eastern

Built by King Akhenaten and Queen Nefertiti, the city of Akhetaten is now known as Amarna.

Meidum

Faiyum

Herakleopolis

Nile River

Akhetaten

Mediterranean Sea

Alexandria

The city of Alexandria was founded by Alexander the Great, and was home to the Ptolemaic kings. Cleopatra VII died in Alexandria in 30 BC.

Saqqara Step Pyramid

LOWER EGYPT

Dahshur Bent Pyramid

Underwater city

Today, much of ancient Alexandria lies under the waters of the Mediterranean Sea. It is being excavated by specialist underwater archaeologists.

Pyramids and tombs at Giza

This desert cemetery site was used by the 4th-Dynasty pyramid builders Menkaure (left), Khaefre (center), and Khufu (right). Many nobles built tombs around the three pyramids.

Karnak temple
The Karnak temple complex includes the temple of Amen, the most important of the New Kingdom gods; the temple of his wife, Mut; and of their son, Khonsu.

Philae Island
The temple of Isis was originally built on the island of Philae. It was moved to the nearby island of Agilqiyya in the early 1970s to save it from the waters of Lake Nasser when the Nile was dammed.

Red Sea

Desert

Egypt's oldest royal cemetery is at Abydos.

The temple of Horus is at Edfu.

The double temple of Sobek and Horus is at Kom Ombo.

Akhmim
Abydos
Dendera
Naqada
Karnak
Luxor (Thebes)
Deir el-Bahri
Esna
Edfu
Kom Ombo
Nile River
Aswan
Elephantine Island
Philae Island
Nubia

Aswan was the traditional southern border of Egypt.

The ancient city of Akhmim is now lost beneath a modern town. It is home to a colossal statue of Princess Meritamen.

UPPER EGYPT

Western Desert

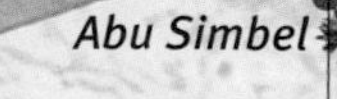
Abu Simbel

King Ramesses II built two magnificent rock-cut temples in the Abu Simbel cliff.

Dendera temple
The temple of Hathor at Dendera was built toward the end of the ancient Egyptian empire. The columns of the temple have Hathor-shaped tops.

Deir el-Bahri temples
The mortuary temple built by the female King Hatshepsut is one of the world's most beautiful buildings. The ruined pyramid-shaped temple-tomb of King Montuhotep II stands nearby.

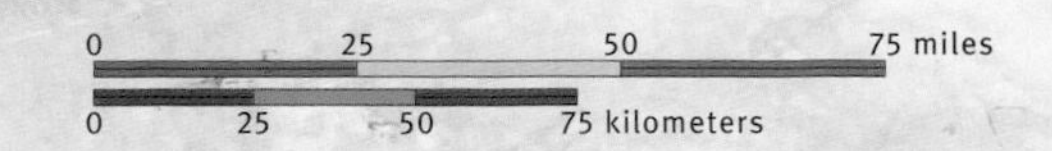

Timeline of Ancient Egypt

Egypt's long history
The Dynastic Age lasted for more than 3,000 years, stretching from the unification of Egypt to the death of Cleopatra VII.

BEFORE EGYPT BECAME ONE LAND

Before Egypt was unified, people lived in independent city-states that traded with each other, using the Nile as a highway.

Quartz figure of the god Horus

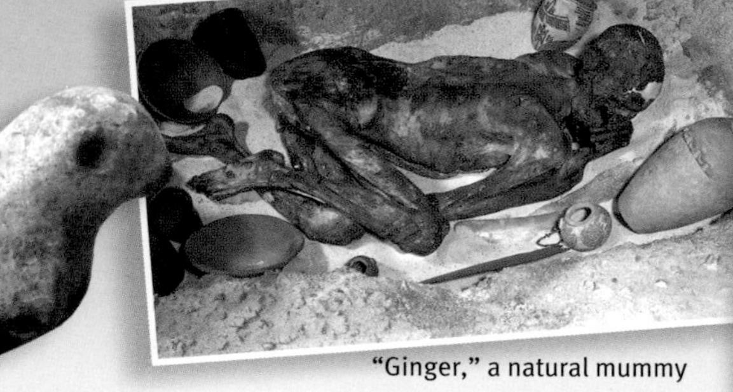

"Ginger," a natural mummy

Ivory figurine

Ostrich egg engraved with cattle

Before 3000 BC PREHISTORIC AND PREDYNASTIC PERIOD — THOUSANDS OF YEARS

DYNASTIES 1–2 UNIFICATION OF EGYPT

The southern warrior Narmer united the city-states and made Egypt one land. Egypt was ruled from the northern city of Memphis. Hieroglyphic writing developed and the first mastaba tombs were built.

Narmer Palette (front and back)

Double crown of Upper and Lower Egypt

Ivory jar label showing early hieroglyphs

The name of King Aha

3000–2649 BC EARLY DYNASTIC PERIOD — 351 YEARS

DYNASTIES 3–6 AGE OF PYRAMIDS

Egypt's kings worshipped the sun god, Re, and built massive stone pyramid tombs in cemeteries in the northern desert. Meanwhile, undertakers were experimenting with different ways of preserving bodies.

Djoser's pyramid at Saqqara

Snefru's pyramid at Meidum

Khufu's pyramid at Giza

Menkaure and his queen

Old Kingdom wooden boat

Nofret, wife of Prince Rahotep

2649–2150 BC OLD KINGDOM — 499 YEARS

2150–2040 BC FIRST INTERMEDIATE PERIOD DYNASTIES 7–11

DYNASTIES 11–14 POLITICAL STABILITY

Art, sculpture, and literature flourished in this time of peace and prosperity. Egypt was ruled from the city of Itj Tawi, which has now completely disappeared.

Mentuhotep II

Senwosret III

Jewelry belonging to Princess Mereret

Amenemhat III as a human-faced sphinx

2040–1640 BC MIDDLE KINGDOM 400 YEARS

Middle Kingdom coffin

1640–1550 BC SECOND INTERMEDIATE PERIOD DYNASTIES 15–17

DYNASTIES 18–20 AGE OF EMPIRE

With extensive eastern and southern empires, Egypt became extremely wealthy. Thebes was the capital city, and kings were buried in rock-cut tombs in the Valley of the Kings.

The female King Hatshepsut

Akhenaten and Nefertiti worship The Aten

Tutankhamen's mummy mask

Temple at Abu Simbel built by Ramesses II

1550–1070 BC NEW KINGDOM 480 YEARS

1070–712 BC THIRD INTERMEDIATE PERIOD DYNASTIES 21–24

DYNASTIES 25–31 LAST EGYPTIAN RULERS

In this confusing time Egypt was ruled by foreign kings from Nubia and from Persia, interspersed with periods of local rule. In 332 BC, Alexander the Great conquered Egypt.

Amasis as a human-headed sphinx

Nectanebo and the goddess Neith

Darius the Great, foreign ruler from the kingdom of Persia

Alexander the Great, foreign ruler from Macedonia

712–332 BC LATE PERIOD 380 YEARS

END OF INDEPENDENCE

Egypt was ruled by a dynasty of Macedonian, or Greek, kings and queens who lived in Alexandria. The death of Cleopatra VII in 30 BC was the end of the Dynastic Age.

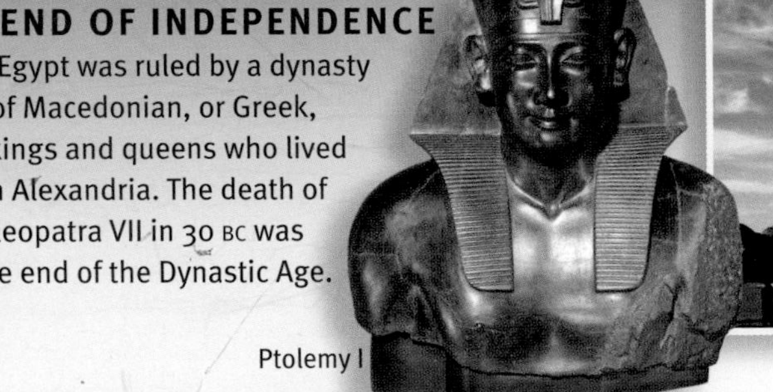

Ptolemy I

Temple of Edfu

Rosetta stone

Cleopatra VII

332–30 BC PTOLEMAIC PERIOD 302 YEARS

END OF THE EMPIRE TO PRESENT DAY

As part of the Roman Empire, Egypt became a Christian country. In AD 640, Egypt was conquered by the Arabs and became a Muslim country. Today, Egypt takes care of its archaeological heritage.

The god Serapis

Inside the Egyptian Museum, Cairo

Cairo, the modern capital, at night

The Koran

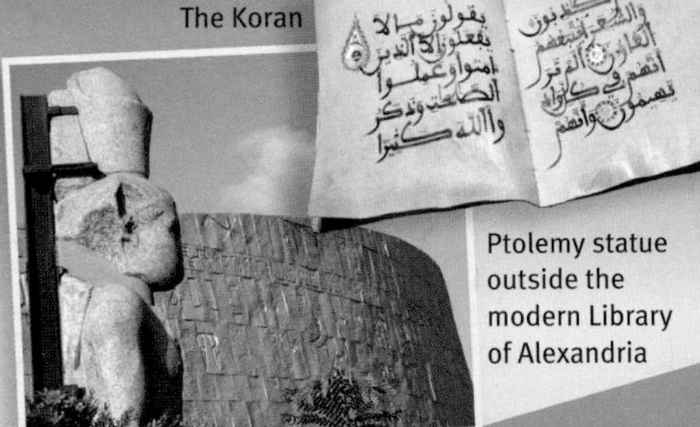

Ptolemy statue outside the modern Library of Alexandria

30 BC–Today FROM THE ROMAN EMPIRE TO PRESENT DAY MORE THAN 2,000 YEARS

Top to bottom

The king stood at the top of Egypt's social pyramid. Beneath him came, in order of importance and wealth, the queen and the queen mother; the royal children; the educated upper classes; the skilled middle classes; the peasants; and finally prisoners of war and criminals. Slavery did exist, but it was rare.

New Kingdom society

Population and social structure varied from period to period in ancient Egypt. As we have no census information, Egyptologists have to base population estimates on a count of graves and tombs.

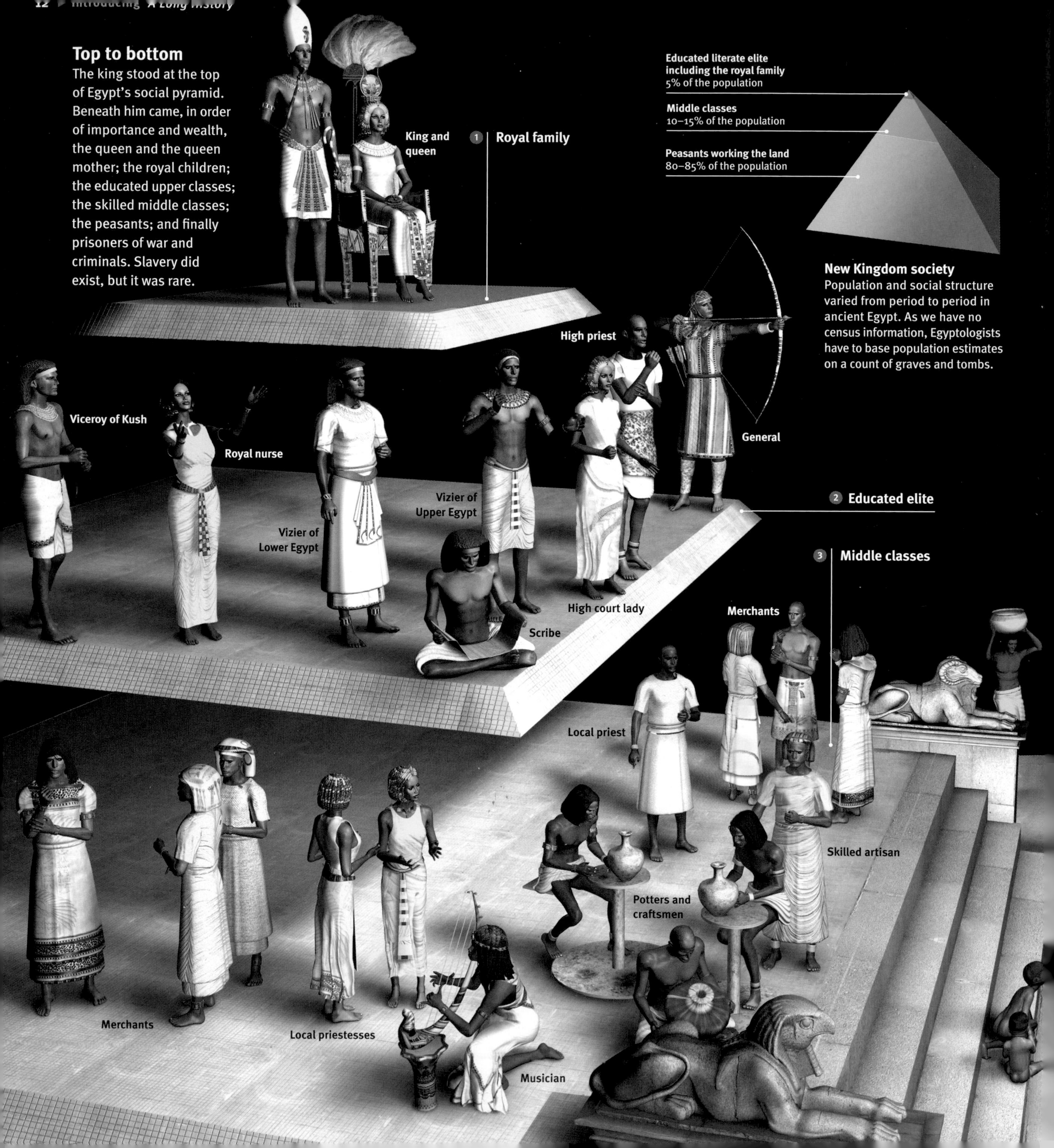

The Ancient Egyptian Social Pyramid

Egypt had a rigid social structure. Boys were trained to do the same work as their fathers and grandfathers, while girls were raised to become good wives and mothers. Women could work outside the home—for example, married women ran market stalls selling off surplus produce—but their domestic duties always took priority. Marriages occurred between a man and a woman of the same social class, and only those lucky enough to receive an education could hope to move up the social pyramid. Egypt was ruled by the king, or pharaoh, the only living Egyptian thought to be able to communicate with the gods. The pharaoh was head of the army, the civil service, and the priesthood. He was assisted in his work by the educated upper classes who lived in cities and had splendid tombs built for them. The vast majority of the population were peasants who worked the land owned by the state and the temples, and who were buried in simple desert graves.

Making mud bricks
This scene from the tomb of the vizier Rekhmire shows workmen making mud bricks. First (left) they take water from a pool to mix with the mud. Then (right) they use wooden molds to shape the bricks, which will be dried in the sun.

The cattle count
This painted wooden model from the tomb of Meket-Re shows herdsmen bringing their cattle to be counted and recorded by scribes and other officials.

Unearthing
Ancient Egypt

The Dynastic Age ended in 30 BC, when Egypt became a part of the Roman Empire. In AD 391 Egypt was converted to Christianity. The old temples were closed, mummification was abandoned, and the hieroglyphic script was lost. In AD 640 the Arab conquest isolated Egypt from the Western world. For more than a thousand years, Egypt's heritage was more or less forgotten. Then, in 1798, French general Napoléon Bonaparte invaded Egypt. His expedition included a group of distinguished scholars eager to investigate Egypt's ruins. The publication of their work inspired others. Archaeologists, such as ex-circus strongman Giovanni Battista Belzoni, started to uncover the ancient monuments, while linguist Jean François Champollion used the writing on the newly discovered Rosetta stone to decipher the hieroglyphic script.

Unlocking ancient code: the Rosetta stone
This stone was the key that unlocked the lost hieroglyphic script. It is carved with three versions of a decree issued by King Ptolemy V in 196 BC. The decree is written twice in the Egyptian language, using the hieroglyphic script (top) and the demotic script (middle), and once in ancient Greek (bottom). Champollion used the ancient Greek to decode the lost Egyptian scripts.

EGYPTOLOGY TODAY

Egyptologists are still working to obtain a full understanding of life and death in ancient Egypt. They use a wide range of skills, including excavation—on land and underwater—scientific investigation, and language work. At all times they are careful to preserve Egypt's cultural heritage.

Phase 1 First, the skull is recreated.

Phase 2 Then muscles and features are modeled.

Phase 3 The priest Nesperennub is reconstructed.

Recreating ancient Egypt

Excavation is just the beginning of the modern Egyptologist's work. The mummy being excavated by Dr. Zahi Hawass (left) will be taken to a laboratory for full medical analysis, which will provide information about age, gender, and health. The mummy's head may be reconstructed using facial modeling and computer technology (as shown above).

A timeline of archaeological discoveries

1798	Napoleon's scholars arrive in Egypt.
1799	The Rosetta stone is discovered.
1816	Belzoni starts to collect pieces for the British Museum.
1822	Champollion decodes the hieroglyphic script.
1858	The National Antiquities Service is established in Egypt.
1880	Flinders Petrie starts to survey the Great Pyramid.
1922	Howard Carter discovers the tomb of Tutankhamen.
1939	Pierre Montet discovers the royal tombs at Tanis.
1992	The underwater survey of ancient Alexandria begins.
1990s	CAT scans and DNA testing of mummies are possible.

Foreign excavation, 1816

In 1816, Giovanni Battista Belzoni employed workmen to drag the giant head known as the "Young Memnon" (actually a broken colossal statue of Ramesses II) from the Ramesseum at Luxor to the banks of the Nile. The statue is today displayed in the British Museum in London. Modern excavators are not permitted to remove their finds from Egypt.

Egyptian Gods

Egypt had an extensive pantheon of state gods and goddesses. These divine beings behaved much like mortal Egyptians. They fell in love, married, had children, and quarreled. Some gods had particular responsibilities. Thoth was the scribe of the gods, while Hathor was the goddess of motherhood, music, and drunkenness. Statues of the gods were worshipped in the temples that dominated Egypt's cities. Only the king and his priests could communicate with the state gods. The ordinary people were not allowed into the inner part of the temple. Instead, they worshipped less important local gods, and many private houses had shrines for ancestor worship.

Atum, the creator
Myths tell how, at the beginning of time, a mound rose out of the sea. Sitting on the mound was the god Atum. He sneezed, and the divine twins Shu and Tefnut were born. Then Atum cried, and mankind grew from his tears.

The cat goddess Bastet
Many people believe that the Egyptians worshipped all cats. That is not true, but the goddess Bastet did take the form of a cat.

Scarab pectoral
This protective amulet was discovered in Tutankhamen's tomb.

Amulets and charms
Amulets and charms were worn to protect the living and the dead from harm. They could be made from metal, stone, glass, or faience, and often took the form of gods or goddesses.

Wedjat eye amulet
The wedjat eye symbolized the eye of the god Re. Egyptians thought the wedjat eye had healing powers and that it protected its wearer. The blue-green color of this amulet was known as the color of life.

Re
Most important god of Old Kingdom Egypt; a sun god

Isis
Wife of Osiris and mother of Horus; a healer and magician

Osiris
God of the dead, also known as the god-king of the afterlife

Horus
Son of Isis and Osiris; linked to Egypt's living king

Thoth
Scribe of the gods; can take the form of an ibis or a baboon

Anubis
Jackal-headed god of cemeteries and mummification

Seth
Mischievous god; brother of Isis and Osiris

Amen
Most important state god of New Kingdom Egypt

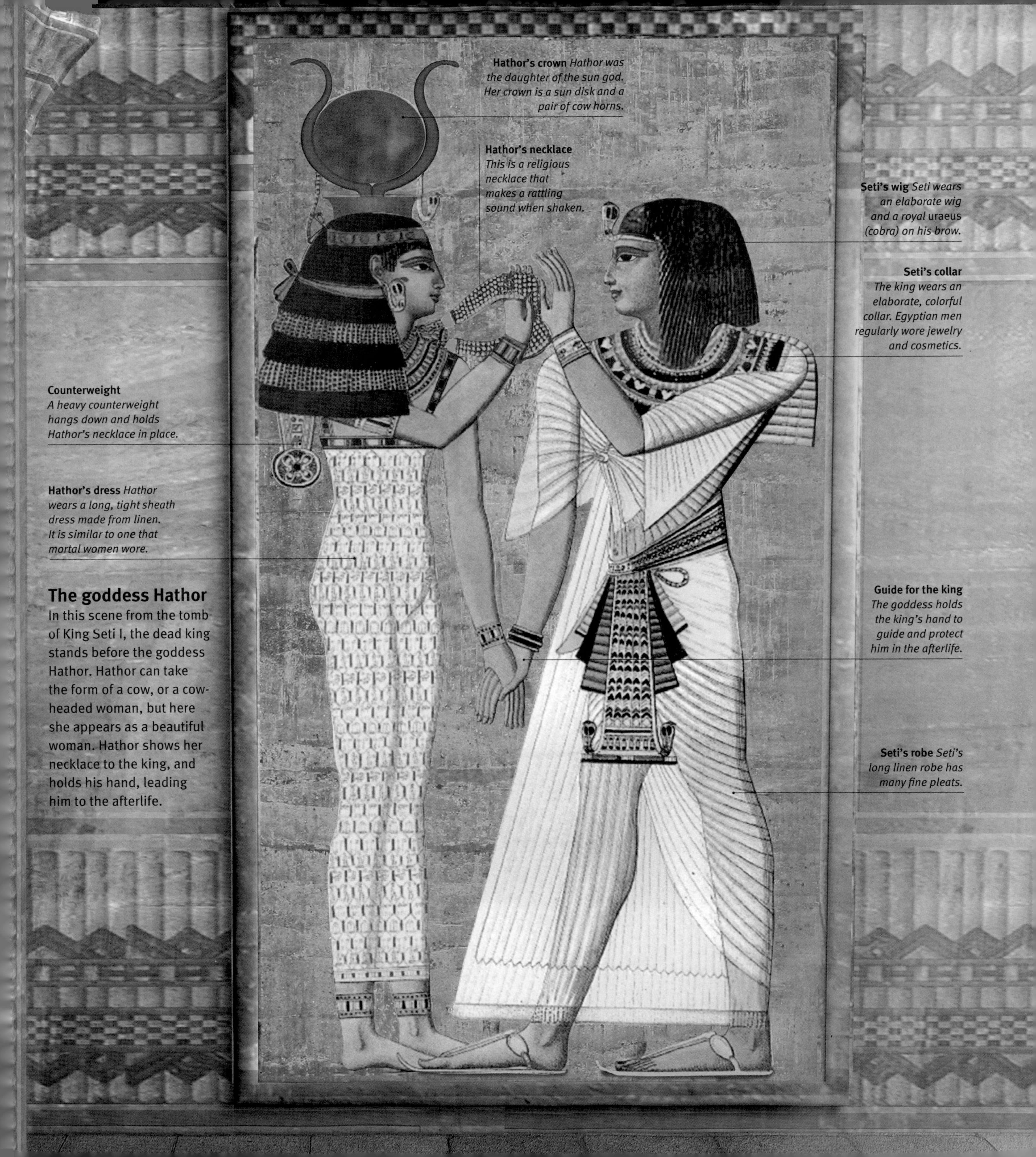

The goddess Hathor

In this scene from the tomb of King Seti I, the dead king stands before the goddess Hathor. Hathor can take the form of a cow, or a cow-headed woman, but here she appears as a beautiful woman. Hathor shows her necklace to the king, and holds his hand, leading him to the afterlife.

Divine Rule of the

Pharaohs

For more than three thousand years a pharaoh, or king, ruled Egypt. The king owned all the land and everything in it. Horus was the god who ruled living Egypt, so a living king was seen as the Horus king. Dead kings were considered to be a form of Osiris, god of the dead. When the living Horus king died, he became an Osiris, and his son and successor became the Horus king. Egypt's kings had one main wife, the queen consort, a woman who played an important role in political and religious matters and who was featured in formal art alongside the king. Often the queen consort was the king's sister. Kings had many secondary wives who lived private lives away from the court.

SYMBOLS OF POWER

Kings of Egypt wore a variety of crowns on different ceremonial occasions. Queens and gods also wore crowns. Although none of Egypt's crowns have survived, archaeologists believe that they were made from leather.

Red crown of Lower Egypt

White crown of Upper Egypt

Double crown of Upper and Lower Egypt

Feathered crown worn by Osiris

Atef crown worn above a headcloth

Blue war crown

Uraeus, or royal cobra, worn on crowns above the brow

Vulture, also worn on crowns just above the brow

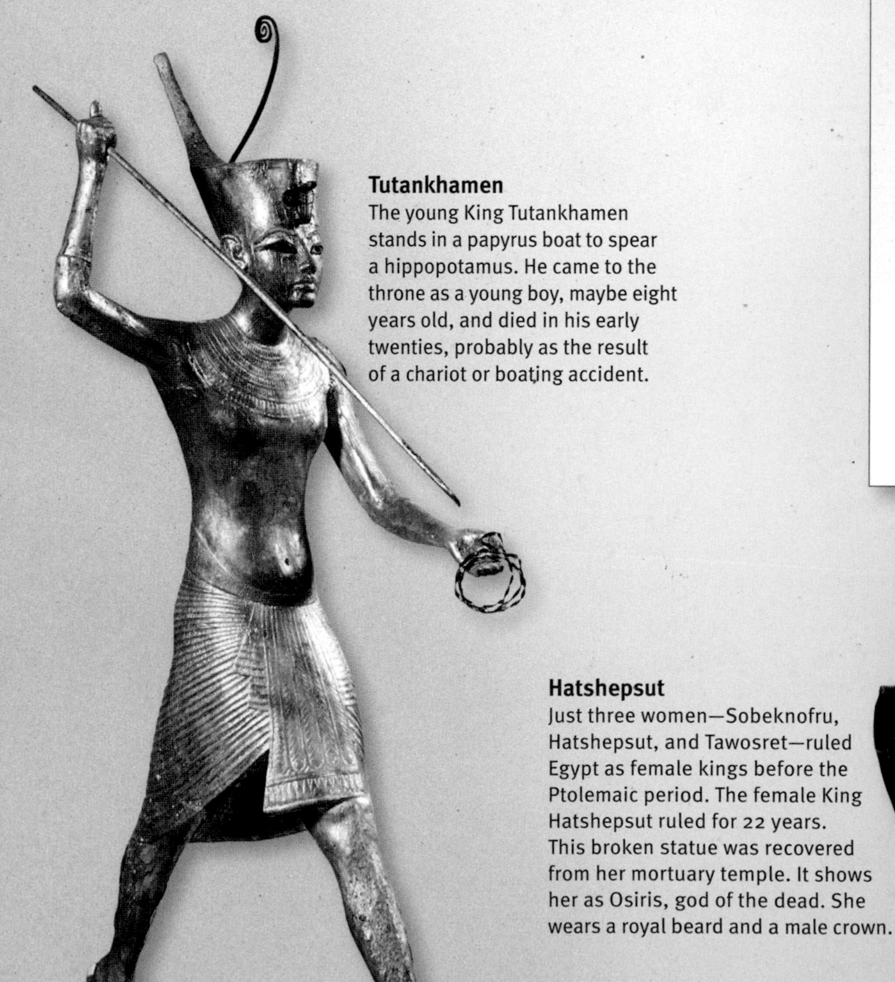

Tutankhamen
The young King Tutankhamen stands in a papyrus boat to spear a hippopotamus. He came to the throne as a young boy, maybe eight years old, and died in his early twenties, probably as the result of a chariot or boating accident.

Hatshepsut
Just three women—Sobeknofru, Hatshepsut, and Tawosret—ruled Egypt as female kings before the Ptolemaic period. The female King Hatshepsut ruled for 22 years. This broken statue was recovered from her mortuary temple. It shows her as Osiris, god of the dead. She wears a royal beard and a male crown.

The king and queen

Pharaohs were always depicted as young, healthy men, even if, as we sometimes see from their unwrapped mummies, they were actually old and unfit. Queens often stood slightly behind their husbands. They were always shown as beautiful and young.

Ceremonial flail *This agricultural tool was carried by kings and the god Osiris.*

White crown *This crown was first worn by the prehistoric Scorpion king, who ruled before Egypt became one united land.*

Jewelry *The king and queen both wore elaborate beaded necklaces.*

Makeup *Both men and women wore extravagant eye makeup.*

Crook *A ceremonial crook was carried by kings and the god Osiris.*

Vulture headdress *The vulture headdress looked like a bird sitting on the queen's head.*

Royal cobra *A uraeus, or royal cobra, is on the front of the queen's vulture headdress.*

Wig *Wealthy women regularly wore wigs. A strand of the queen's own hair, from beneath her wig, can be seen against her face.*

Dress *The queen wore pleated dresses made from fine linen.*

Kilt *The king's kilt was made of white linen that was produced from the flax plant.*

Building the Pyramids

The kings of the Old and Middle kingdoms built pyramid tombs in cemeteries in the northern desert. The earliest pyramids were made of stone; the later ones were built of mud brick disguised with a thin stone casing. Many of these later pyramids have since collapsed. Not all pyramids had the same internal plan. Some included a burial chamber within the pyramid itself. Others were built above a burial chamber that was cut into the ground. Pyramid building required a large workforce at the pyramid site and in the quarries. Some of these workers were full-time professional pyramid builders, but most were laborers who were summoned to work for the king for three months, then sent home again.

An astounding achievement

No one knows exactly how many blocks of stone were included in Egypt's pyramids, but it has been estimated that the Great Pyramid may have included as many as 2.3 million blocks weighing on average 2.5 tons (2.3 t). The stone for the pyramid interior was obtained from quarries close by the building site. Better-quality limestone was used for the exterior of the pyramid.

High-quality stone *Fine limestone blocks have come by boat from a quarry across the Nile. They will be used for the pyramid's outer casing.*

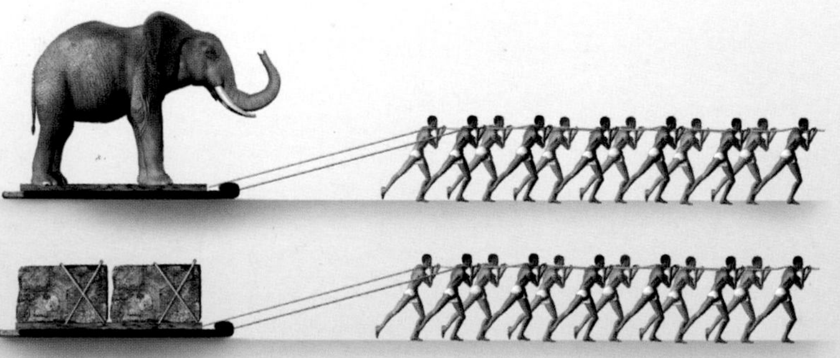

Pyramid stones
Experts estimate that two stone blocks could have weighed as much as one elephant. Blocks were dragged from nearby quarries on wooden sledges.

HOW TALL WERE THE PYRAMIDS?

Until the 19th century, Khufu's Great Pyramid was the tallest building in the world. Equivalent to a modern 48-story building, its height of 481 feet (146 m) has been surpassed by skyscrapers such as Taipei 101 in Taiwan, which reaches 1,667 feet (508 m). The Great Pyramid, however, is still the most massive building ever constructed—you could build 30 Empire State Buildings with its limestone blocks.

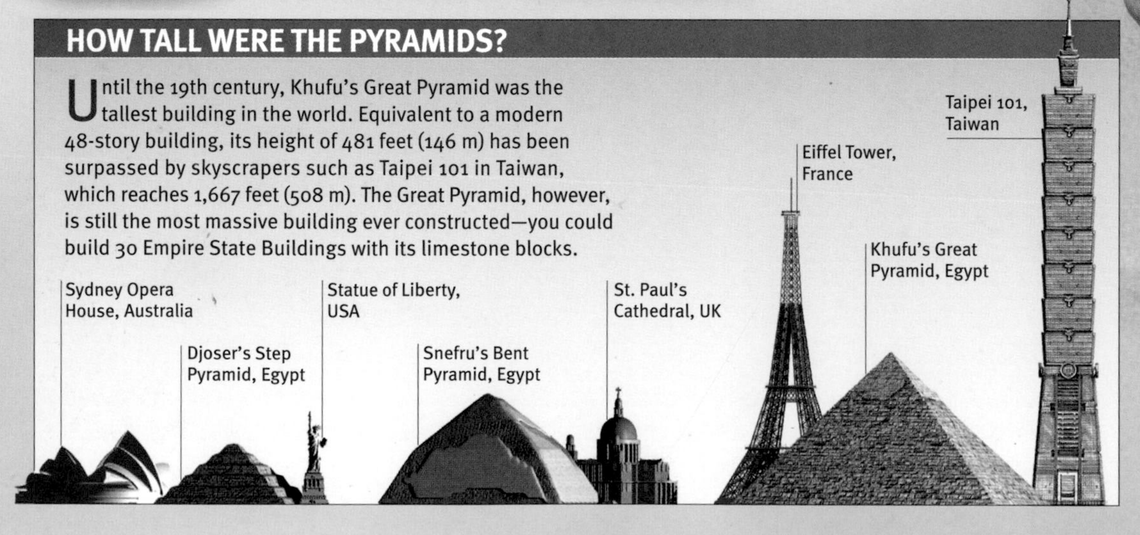

Water carriers *Men and donkeys carry water to the roadway. Water is poured onto the roadway to help the stones slide along.*

Ramps
Pyramid builders used mud and rubble ramps that were dismantled when the pyramid was complete. There were several possible ramp styles.

Straight ramp

Zigzag ramp up one face

Straight ramp with a wraparound zigzag ramp

Roadway *The roadway is made from heavy wooden beams set into the ground.*

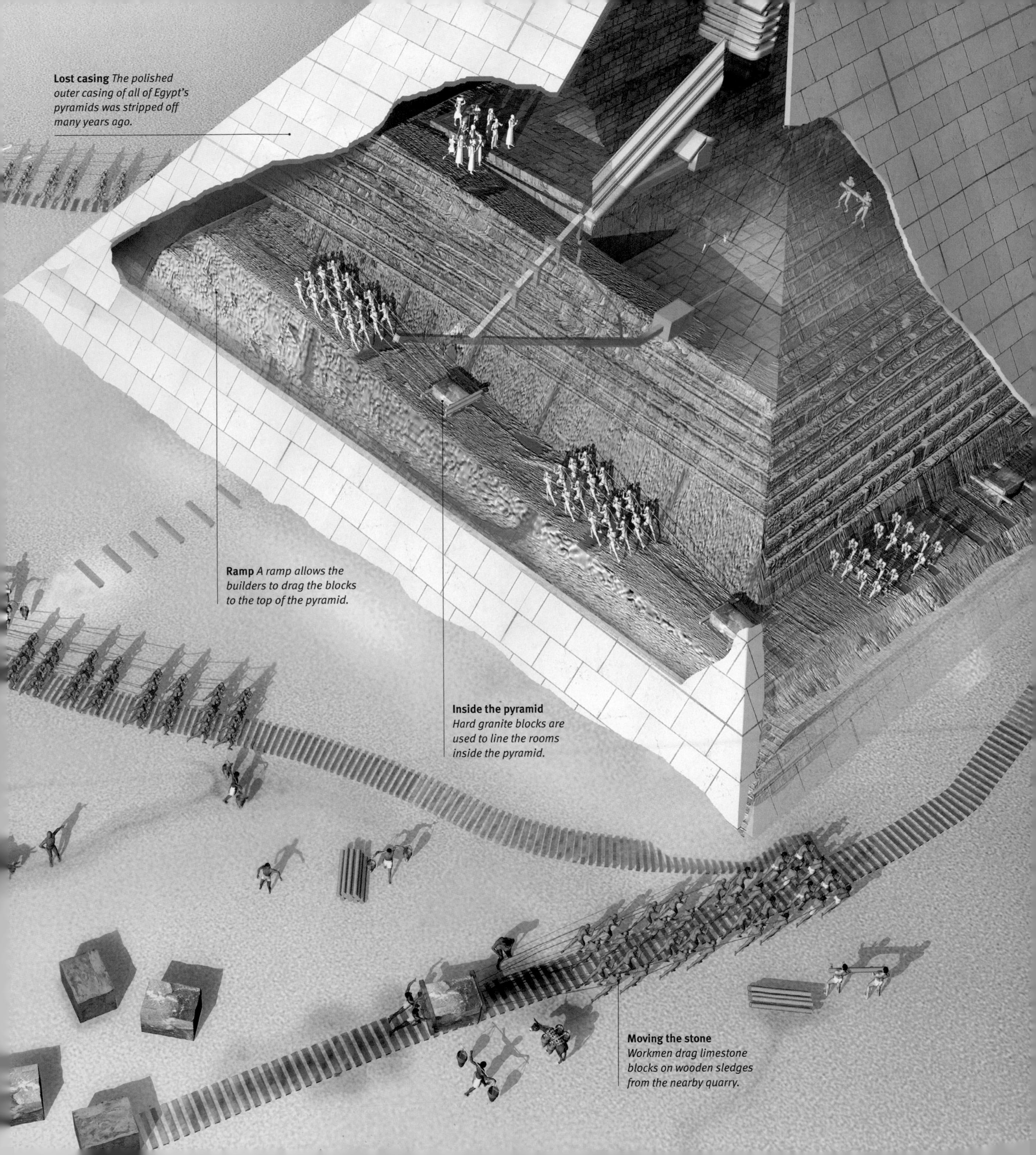
Lost casing *The polished outer casing of all of Egypt's pyramids was stripped off many years ago.*
Ramp *A ramp allows the builders to drag the blocks to the top of the pyramid.*
Inside the pyramid *Hard granite blocks are used to line the rooms inside the pyramid.*
Moving the stone *Workmen drag limestone blocks on wooden sledges from the nearby quarry.*

The Making of a Mummy

A mummy is a preserved body. The first Egyptian mummies occurred naturally, when bodies buried in the hot desert sands dried out. Without moisture, the bacteria that cause decay could not survive, and the bodies did not rot. Inspired by these natural mummies, the Egyptians believed that the soul could live forever as long as the body was preserved. For almost 3,000 years wealthy Egyptians mummified their dead. The elaborate process was carried out by priests and took about 70 days.

Wrapping begins *After embalming, the head is the first part of the mummy to be wrapped in linen bandages.*

Returning organs *At different times, the dried-out organs are wrapped in linen and returned to the body, or preserved in canopic jars.*

Jewelry and charms *Jewelry and amulets (lucky charms, often inscribed with spells) are inserted into the linen wrappings.*

Throwaway brain *Considered unimportant, the brain is removed from the skull through the nose and thrown away.*

Gods and rituals *Anubis, the jackal-headed god, watches over the embalming process, which involves special rituals at each stage.*

Preserving organs *The intestines, liver, stomach, and lungs are removed through a slit in the left side of the body. These organs are then covered in a salt called natron to dry them out.*

Treasured heart *The heart remains in the body. Ancient Egyptians believed the heart was the center of intelligence.*

Lake salt *Natron is a deposit found on the shores of salt lakes. It is spread over the body and left there for 40 days to dry it out. Once all moisture has been removed, the body will not decay.*

On a slope *The slanted embalming table allows body fluids to drip away as the body dries out.*

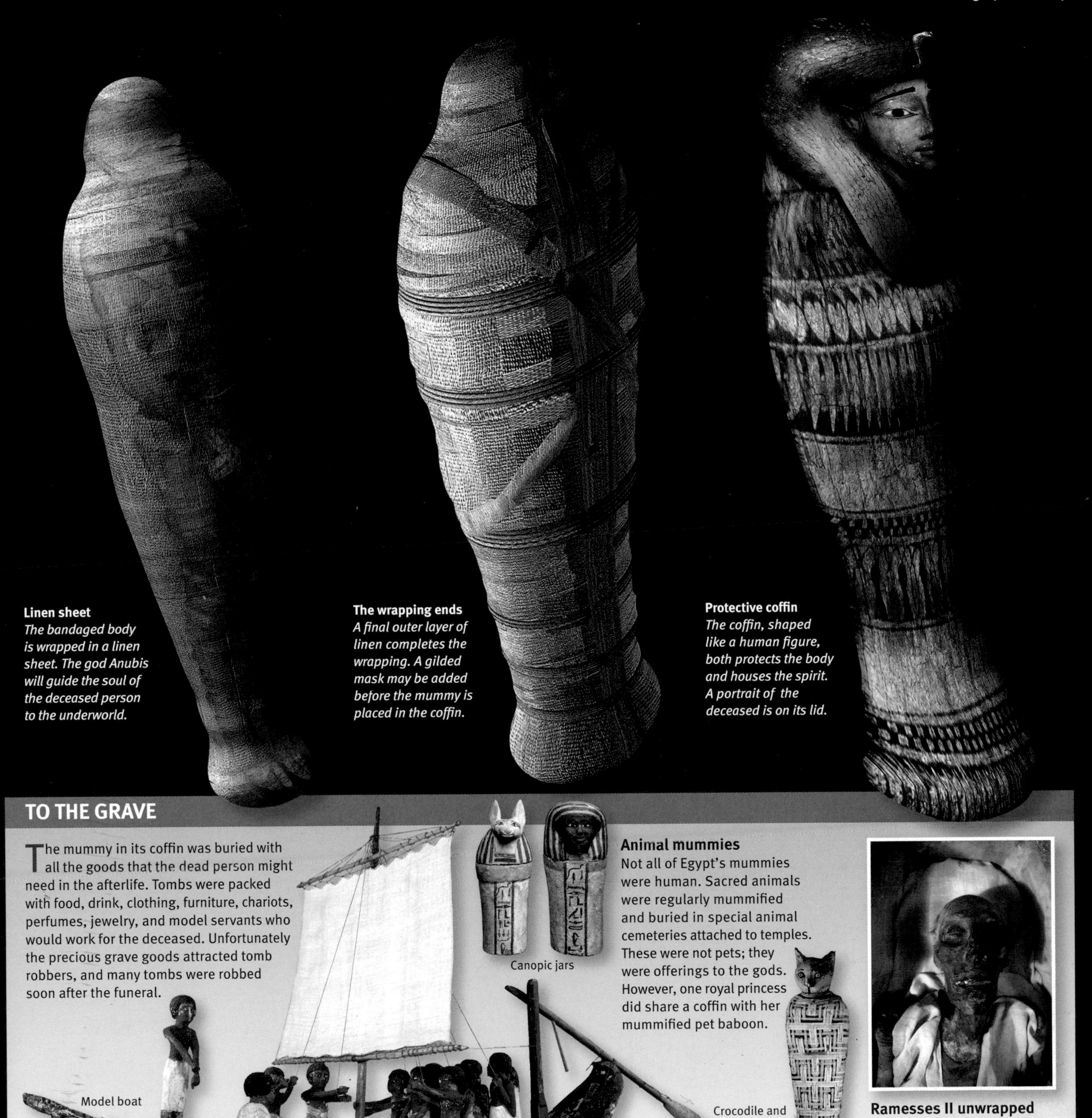

Linen sheet
The bandaged body is wrapped in a linen sheet. The god Anubis will guide the soul of the deceased person to the underworld.

The wrapping ends
A final outer layer of linen completes the wrapping. A gilded mask may be added before the mummy is placed in the coffin.

Protective coffin
The coffin, shaped like a human figure, both protects the body and houses the spirit. A portrait of the deceased is on its lid.

TO THE GRAVE

The mummy in its coffin was buried with all the goods that the dead person might need in the afterlife. Tombs were packed with food, drink, clothing, furniture, chariots, perfumes, jewelry, and model servants who would work for the deceased. Unfortunately the precious grave goods attracted tomb robbers, and many tombs were robbed soon after the funeral.

Model boat

Canopic jars

Animal mummies
Not all of Egypt's mummies were human. Sacred animals were regularly mummified and buried in special animal cemeteries attached to temples. These were not pets; they were offerings to the gods. However, one royal princess did share a coffin with her mummified pet baboon.

Crocodile and cat mummies

Ramesses II unwrapped
Ramesses II's unwrapped mummy shows he was tall, with a large nose and red hair.

ourney to the Afterlife

deas about the afterlife changed throughout the Dynastic Age. At first only the king had a soul strong enough to leave he tomb and live with the gods. Everyone else had to exist s a ghost inside their tomb. During the Middle Kingdom, deas about the afterlife became more democratic and, as ong as the correct rituals were performed, any soul could eave its tomb and live with Osiris in the Field of Reeds the afterlife). During an Egyptian funeral, mourners were ired to weep and cover their heads with dust. A priest erformed the "opening of the mouth ceremony" at the tomb loor, touching the face of the mummy with sacred tools. This itual allowed the soul of the deceased to return to life. The oul then journeyed into the west, where he or she would pass hrough a maze and answer questions posed by demon gatekeepers. Finally, the deceased would be judged by Osiris.

ervants for the afterlife
Worried that they might have to work in the Field of Reeds, wealthy gyptians were buried with model ervants known as *shabtis*. They ooked like miniature mummies, and ome carried baskets or farming tools. *habtis* were inscribed with a spell hat brought them to life.

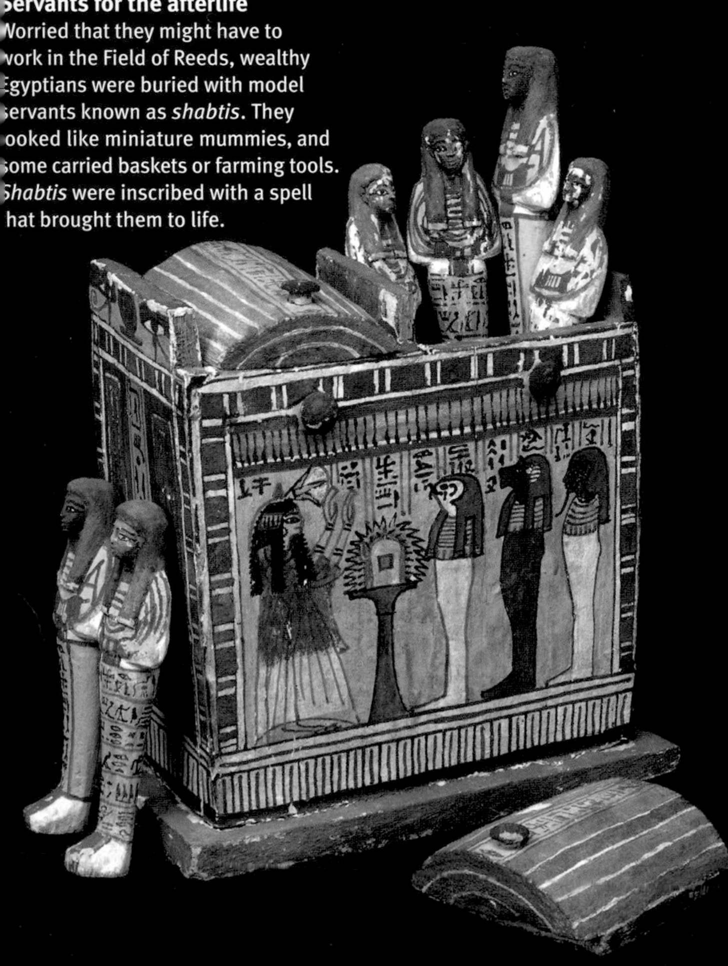

Hunefer's journey *The jackel-headed god Anubis leads the dead Hunefer toward the hall of judgment. In his left hand Anubis holds the* ankh *sign of life.*

Weighing the heart *Hunefer's heart is weighed against the feather of truth.*

Anubis *Anubis adjusts the scales to make sure they are accurate.*

The *Book of the Dead*

The *Book of the Dead* was a religious text that was written either on tomb walls or on a papyrus scroll. It told the deceased how to behave in the afterlife, and it illustrated the various stages of the journey toward the Field of Reeds. This version of the *Book of the Dead* belongs to a man named Hunefer.

Osiris *Osiris, god of the dead, watches the judgment of Hunefer from his throne.*
"Opening of the mouth ceremony" *Horus performs this important ceremony, which will allow the dead soul to come back to life.*
Anubis the jackal *God of the cemetery, Anubis can appear either as a jackal (as on the top of this chest) or as a jackal-headed man (as on the front of the chest).*
Sarcophagus *Inside this large wooden sarcophagus, or outer coffin, the mummy is stored within more human-shaped coffins.*
Thoth *As scribe of the gods, Thoth records the result in his papyrus scroll. The heart is found to be light.*
Canopic chest *The canopic chest holds four canopic jars that contain the preserved stomach, intestines, liver, and lungs.*
Ammit *The beast Ammit waits next to the scales. He will eat Hunefer if his heart weighs more than the feather.*
Horus *The god Horus leads Hunefer to the throne of Osiris. The four miniature figures are the four sons of Horus.*

Working the Land

Egypt's three seasons were named after the predictable rise and fall of the Nile. Every year, from July to October, the Nile swelled and burst its banks, spreading water and fertile soil over the fields. This season was "Akhet," the time of flooding. At the end of the season, in late October, the retreat of the river waters left fields moist and ready for planting. The next season, "Peret," which corresponded to winter (November to March), was the time of coming forth. Peret ended with a bountiful harvest. In summer, or "Shemu" (April to June), the hot sun baked the land and sterilized the soil. This natural agricultural rhythm came to an end in the 1960s when the Aswan High Dam was built.

Egypt's farmers

Egypt owed its economic success to its hardworking farmers. The vast majority of the population lived in hamlets and villages, on farmland owned by the wealthy minority. Surplus food was stored in warehouses attached to the temples and palaces.

Sowing the crops *Retreating floodwaters left the fields moist and soft and covered in dying fish that the farmers could gather and eat. Quickly, before the ground hardened, farmers scattered seed and plowed it into the soil.*

The time of flooding *The season of Akhet left the fields underwater and the farmers short of work, although kings could often find tasks for their idle workforce. Sensibly, the farmers built their mud-brick houses out of reach of the floodwaters.*

Houses safe from floodwaters

The Nile floods fields.

Agriculture in the afterlife

Many wealthy Egyptians decorated their tombs with agricultural scenes. These were not scenes of the life they had lived in Egypt, but idealized scenes of fertile fields and rich harvests that they expected to enjoy after death.

Bountiful harvest *After a winter spent scaring birds away from the fields, farmers were ready to harvest their crops. Egypt's farmers grew wheat and barley to eat, and flax to spin into linen thread for clothing. Legumes, fruit, and vegetables were grown in market gardens.*

Farmers harvesting crops

Wheat and barley are grown to make bread and beer.

LATE PERET

Boats on the Nile

The Nile was the main highway through ancient Egypt, linking the towns and cities that sprawled along its banks. More distant sites, such as desert pyramids, were linked to the Nile by a system of canals. The Egyptians had no road network and they depended on boats as their main form of transport. Although few actual boats survive, illustrations and models tell us about the various types of vessels. The first Egyptian boats were made from papyrus and appeared about 4000 BC. Larger, more expensive wooden boats were used by the royal family and carried trade goods across the Mediterranean Sea. Enormous wooden barges, towed by fleets of smaller boats, were used to move heavy building materials and colossal stone statues.

Papyrus raft
The first boat on the Nile was made from papyrus reeds bound together with ropes. Cheap and easy to make, it was used for river crossings and for fishing and hunting. It is often shown in paintings carrying the sun god.

Old Kingdom
Wood replaced papyrus as the main boat-building material for large boats during the Old Kingdom. Some boats were strong enough to transport many tons of stone from the quarries in Upper Egypt to the site of the pyramids.

Middle Kingdom
In the Middle Kingdom, hull design became less heavy-beamed and more round-bottomed. The sail could be raised when traveling upstream with the wind, and lowered when rowing downstream with the current.

BOAT BUILDING

While the ancient Egyptians based the design of their wooden boats on their earlier papyrus vessels, they also borrowed a number of boat-building techniques from their trading partners.

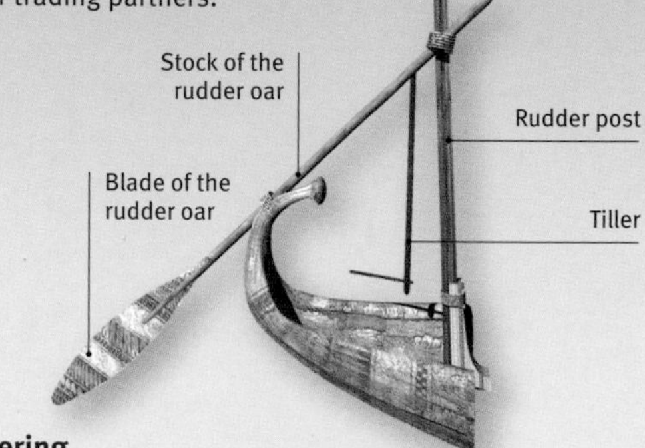

Steering
Most Middle Kingdom boats had a single massive rudder oar. A helmsman would stand between the rudder post and oar, moving the tiller sideways to rotate the oar and steer the boat.

Planking
The hull and sides of wooden boats were built without any nails. A scarcity of high-quality wood meant that many boats were made from short planks. The planks were joined by wooden butterfly cramps and dowels, or lashed together with ropes. Wood for larger boats was imported.

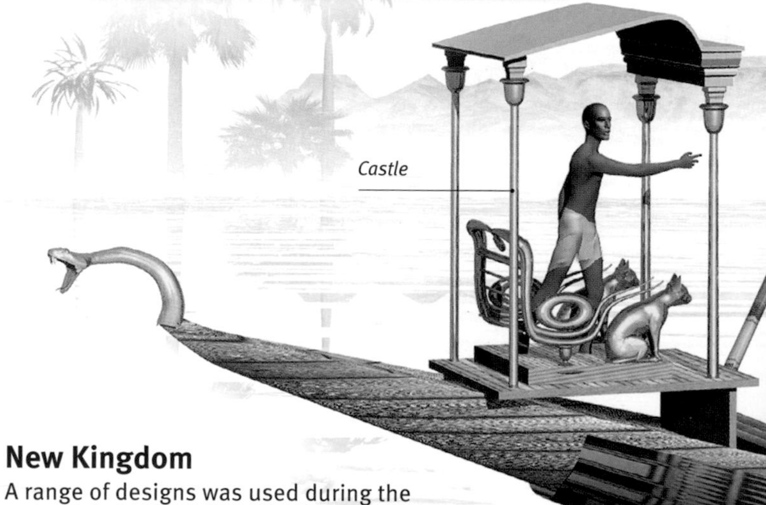

New Kingdom

A range of designs was used during the New Kingdom, but they usually featured two rudder oars, a central deckhouse, and a castle at either end for passengers. Cargo was carried in the deckhouse and on the open deck.

Rudder oar
Mast
Deckhouse
Linen sail
Castle

An Egyptian Household

Although the ancient Egyptians built their tombs and temples from stone, they built their houses and palaces with mud brick. Mud brick was cheap, readily available, and kept houses warm in winter and cool in the hot summer months. Unfortunately, while many temples and tombs have survived, almost all the mud-brick houses have crumbled and vanished. Archaeologists are therefore forced to rely on ground plans, and on ancient drawings, when trying to reconstruct Egyptian houses.

A nobleman's villa

This villa has been reconstructed from a tomb-drawing. While the poorer members of society lived in small, cramped terraced houses, wealthy Egyptians built extensive villas like this one. Outside the villa there were peaceful gardens and a pool teeming with fish.

Granaries

Djehuty-nefer, the master of the house

Living room

Reception room

Servants prepare food and drink, such as bread and beer.

Kitchen

SINGLE OR MULTISTORY HOUSES?

Tomb-drawings suggest the Egyptians lived in multistory houses, but archaeological discoveries indicate that they lived in extensive single-story houses. Why this difference? It may be that Egyptian artists, eager to show all the rooms in a house but unable to create a perspective drawing, illustrated the rooms one on top of another.

Central living room

Pillared reception room

Steps leading to door and vestibule

Bedroom

Bathroom

Bedroom

Archaeological evidence suggests this nobleman's house was a single-story villa (above), even though a tomb-drawing shows it as a multistory dwelling (left).

Precious furniture

The Egyptians took their furniture to the grave. This ancient low chair, stool, and table were recovered from a New Kingdom Theban tomb.

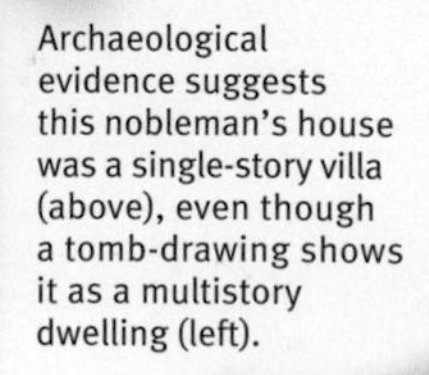

Storage bins and grain silos
Food and vessels are carried up to the granary.
Although these arches look like windows in the tomb-drawing, they were probably storage vessels of some sort.
Bedrooms and bathrooms may have been to the right of this staircase. This area of the tomb-drawing was damaged, but archaeological evidence suggests Egyptian houses had bathrooms with toilets and showers.
Servants take produce to be inspected by their master and recorded by scribes.
Guests are received in the reception room.
Servants carry food through the antechamber.
Possible servants' quarters

Singing, Dancing, and

Making Music

Music and dance played an important role in Egyptian daily life from the earliest of times. There were no theaters or concert halls, but musicians entertained at private banquets and at religious festivals, while three different types of dances were included in the elaborate funeral service. Tomb illustrations show that many of the dances were athletic, including back flips and even cartwheels. While most Egyptian women wore long dresses, female dancers wore short garments and even performed naked. Many musical instruments have survived, but as we have no written music it is difficult to reconstruct the sound made by the ancient musicians.

Dance
Many New Kingdom tombs include banqueting scenes that show the diners being entertained by dancing girls and female musicians.

Five-stringed harp

Musical instruments
Egypt's musicians played stringed instruments, such as harps, lutes, and lyres; woodwind instruments, such as flutes, double clarinets, and double oboes; and percussion instruments including tambourines. Some instruments had particular functions. The army used trumpets, bugles, and drums, while rattles, cymbals, and bells were used in religious ceremonies.

Thirteen-stringed harp

Harps Harps were made of wood, inlaid with bone and faience, and painted in bright colors.

The royal harem

The women of the royal harem were accomplished musicians and dancers, who used their skills to entertain the king. Other female musicians and dancers performed at religious ceremonies, and to accompany funerals.

Decorating the tombs

The artists who decorated Egypt's tombs were respected as master craftsmen. This artist uses a grid of horizontal and vertical lines to ensure that his figures have the correct proportions. When he has completed the scene, he will paint over the grid.

Tools of the trade
The artist uses thin reed paintbrushes and paints made from ground pigments.

Pictures of the Past

Ancient Arts

Hieroglyphic writing appeared in Egypt at the beginning of the Dynastic Age in approximately 3100 BC. Hieroglyphs were elaborate signs arranged in rows or columns, which could be read from either left to right or right to left. The earliest writings were long lists closely linked to funerary rituals; they record details of grave goods and offerings to be made to the dead. The first fictional stories were written during the Middle Kingdom. Few Egyptian children attended school, and less than 10 percent of the population could read and write. Schooling for scribes was very dull. Trainee scribes learned to write by copying out, over and over again, texts which included prayers, model letters, stories, and instructions that offered the young scholars advice on how to live a good life.

The royal family relaxes
King Akhenaten and his queen, Nefertiti, play with their daughters. The hieroglyphs surrounding the royal couple explain the scene. The royal names are written in oval loops known as "cartouches."

A	Vulture, Arm	I	Reed	Q	Hillside	Y	Double reed
B	Foot	J	Snake	R	Mouth	Z	No "Z"
C	No "C"	K	Basket	S	Fold of cloth, Door bolt	CH	Ropes
D	Hand	L	Lion	T	Loaf	KH	Placenta
E	Reed	M	Owl	U	Quail chick	SH	Lake
F	Horned cobra	N	Water	V	Horned cobra		
G	Pot stand	O	Lasso	W	Quail chick, Rope coil		
H	Twisted flax, Reed hut	P	Stool	X	No "X"		

The hieroglyphic "alphabet"
The hieroglyphic script is not a simple alphabet, but some of the signs can be translated into our own letters. Why not try writing your own name in hieroglyphs?

THE HIERATIC SCRIPT

Hieratic is a shorter, speedier version of the hieroglyphic script that requires fewer pen strokes. It is always read from right to left. While temples, tombs, and official inscriptions used the traditional hieroglyphs, less formal documents were written in hieratic (as shown below).

Scribe in action
This statue shows an Old Kingdom scribe sitting cross-legged with his papyrus "paper" stretched across his lap. He writes with a thin paintbrush and ink.

Craft and Artifacts

Egypt's craftsmen were respected throughout the ancient world. Jewelers worked with gold, silver, and a wide range of colored semi-precious stones to create necklaces, bracelets, rings, and earrings for both men and women. Bead necklaces were the most common, and presumably cheapest, form of jewelry. They were made from faience and often painted with an eye to represent the eye of Horus and protect the wearer. Stone workers used a variety of hard and soft stone to create beautiful statues and thin-walled stone vessels. Egypt's carpenters suffered from a shortage of wood—there were few tall trees, and high-quality wood had to be imported from Lebanon—yet managed to create ships, coffins, and furniture inlaid with ebony and ivory.

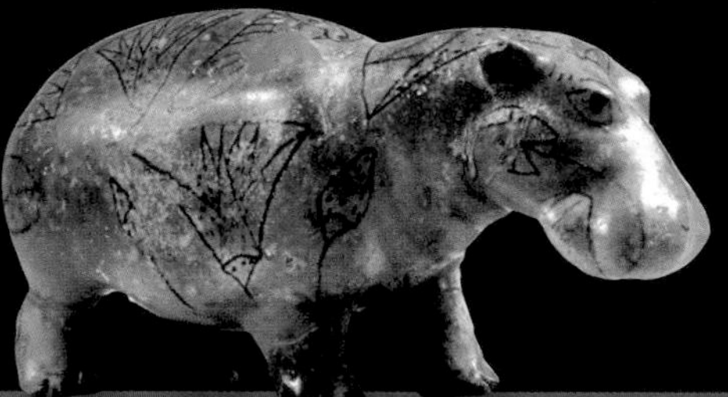

Faience hippopotamus
Faience is an artificial ceramic material made from ground quartz or sand and covered with a distinctive blue or green glaze. It was used to make beads, containers, dishes, and ornaments.

MODEL CRAFTSMEN

Our information about Egypt's craft-working techniques comes from scenes of daily life included on tomb walls, and from Middle Kingdom wooden models made for the tomb. The examination of surviving objects can also help experts to determine just how something was made.

Carpentry workshop
This model, found in the Middle Kingdom tomb of Meket-Re, shows a carpentry workshop. In the middle of the workshop a carpenter is using a metal saw to split a plank of wood.

Ancient medals *Gold flies were the ancient equivalent of medals. They were awarded to brave soldiers.*

Faience bowl
This New Kingdom faience bowl is decorated with a central pool and flowering lotus plants.

Flower-shaped vessel
An alabaster vessel in the form of a half-opened lotus flower was found in Tutankhamen's tomb.

Egyptian jewelry

Egypt obtained gold from the desert mines and from Nubia (modern Sudan). Set with colorful semi-precious stones, such as lapis lazuli, amethyst, carnelian, and turquoise, Egyptian jewelry made a dazzling display against the plain white garments. Silver was rarer than gold, and so more expensive. Poorer Egyptians wore jewelry made from faience and from cheaper stones.

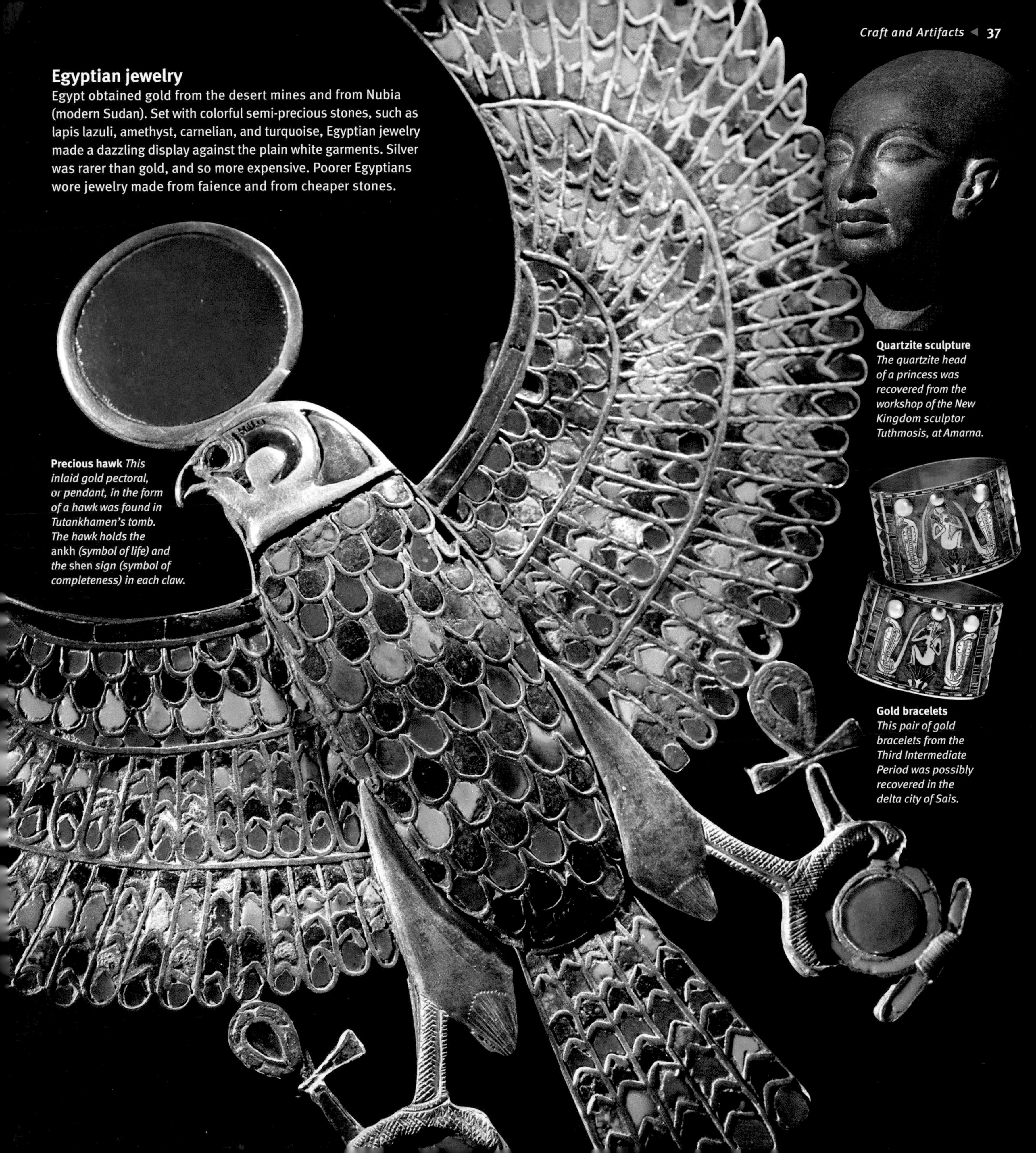

Precious hawk *This inlaid gold pectoral, or pendant, in the form of a hawk was found in Tutankhamen's tomb. The hawk holds the* ankh *(symbol of life) and the* shen *sign (symbol of completeness) in each claw.*

Quartzite sculpture *The quartzite head of a princess was recovered from the workshop of the New Kingdom sculptor Tuthmosis, at Amarna.*

Gold bracelets *This pair of gold bracelets from the Third Intermediate Period was possibly recovered in the delta city of Sais.*

Expanding the Empire

Egypt's Army

Although the king maintained a small royal bodyguard, Old Kingdom Egypt did not have a permanent army. If troops were needed, untrained men were simply summoned from the villages. During the Middle Kingdom the army became a professional fighting force. The soldiers wore no armor but carried long leather shields. They fought on foot, armed with battle-axes, spears, and daggers. Bows and arrows provided long-range coverage. The army expanded during the New Kingdom, as Egypt established and maintained a large empire.

A model army
These painted wooden soldiers were recovered from the Middle Kingdom Asyut tomb of Mesehti. The soldiers carry long shields and spears but have no armor.

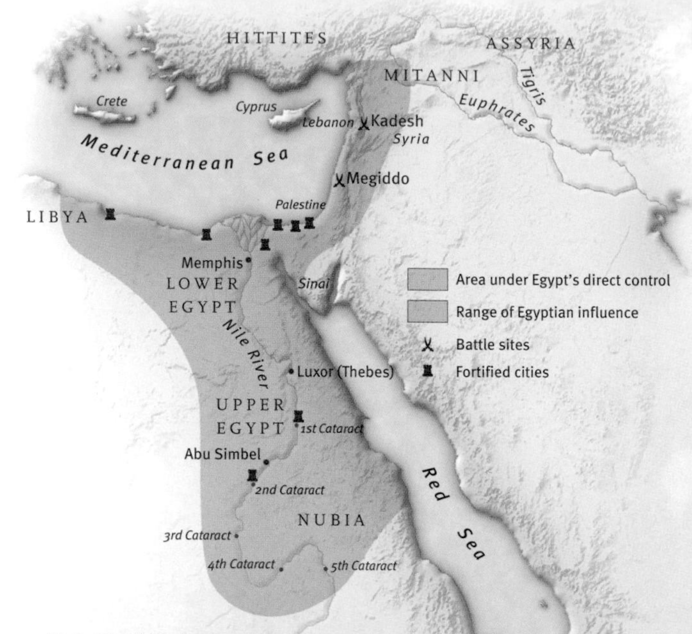

Height of the empire
During the New Kingdom, Egypt expanded its empire. The extent of the empire is shown above in brown. The area that Egypt directly controlled is shown above in green.

Horses *Horses may have worn textured blankets into battle. They had no armor.*

THE EGYPTIAN ARSENAL

Egypt's first hunters and warriors used the "simple" or "self bow" to fire flint- or metal-tipped arrows. The introduction of the more sophisticated "compound bow" at the beginning of the New Kingdom gave soldiers greater range and accuracy.

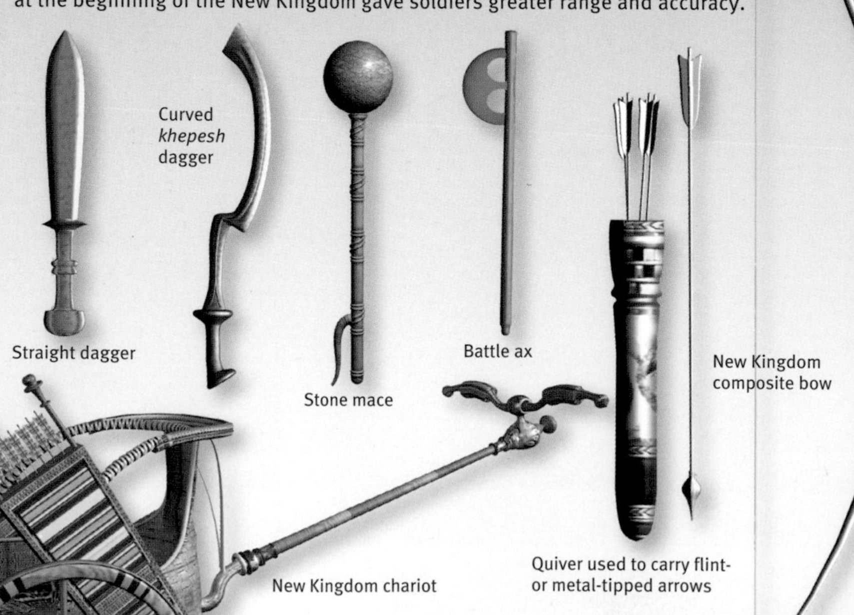

The battle of Kadesh

The Egyptian army had marched out of Egypt to fight the Hittite army. One night two strangers were captured. The strangers told King Ramesses that the Hittites were many miles away. But the strangers were spies. The Hittites were waiting to ambush the Egyptians at the city of Kadesh.

The next day, two more strangers were captured. Ramesses realized that they were spies, and that the Hittites were nearby. Soon the Egyptians were completely surrounded. The Egyptian soldiers ran away, leaving the king and his shield bearer alone. Ramesses prayed to the god Amen and gained strength. Ruthlessly he attacked. By nightfall all the Hittites were either dead or had run away.

Leading the charge *Kings were regularly depicted alone in chariots, with the reins tied around their waist. In reality, they would have had drivers, as shown.*

Riding into battle *Elite soldiers rode to battle in light horse-drawn chariots manned by a driver and a fighter armed with a short shield, spear, and bow.*

Royal armor *The king probably wore armor made from leather scales, and sandals on his feet.*

Charioteer *A driver controlled the chariot while the king used his weapons.*

Locator map This map of Egypt shows you exactly where the featured site is located. Look for the large red dot on each map.

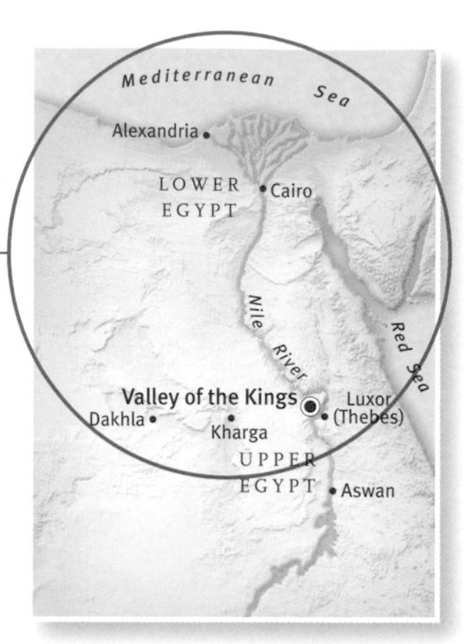

VALLEY OF THE KINGS: THE FACTS

WHEN IT WAS BUILT: New Kingdom, 18th–20th Dynasties, 1550–1070 BC

WHERE IT WAS BUILT: Western Thebes

WHO BUILT IT: Theban kings of the New Kingdom

SIZE: There are two clusters of royal tombs, one in the main valley, and one in the western valley (an offshoot). Put together, the two main areas come to significantly less than one square mile (2.6 sq km)

WHEN IT WAS DISCOVERED: Site was known since ancient times, but many tombs were discovered from 1817 to 1922

CLAIM TO FAME: Burial ground of many of the most famous kings, including Hatshepsut, Tuthmosis III, Tutankhamen, Seti I, and Ramesses II

Fast facts Fast facts at your fingertips give you essential information on each site being explored.

Time bar This time bar shows when the site was constructed and used. The bar stretches from Old Kindgom Egypt to the Late Period.

in focus

2649 BC
OLD KINGDOM
2150 BC
2040 BC
MIDDLE KINGDOM
1640 BC
1550 BC
NEW KINGDOM
1070 BC
712 BC
LATE PERIOD
332 BC

STEP PYRAMID: THE FACTS

WHEN IT WAS BUILT: Old Kingdom, 3rd Dynasty, 2630–2611 BC

WHERE IT WAS BUILT: Saqqara

WHO BUILT IT: The architect Imhotep for King Djoser

SIZE: 205 ft (62.5 m) tall; base length 358 x 397 ft (109 x 121 m)

WHEN IT WAS DISCOVERED: Always known. Surrounding structures excavated since 1924 by Cecil Firth and Jean-Philippe Lauer

CLAIM TO FAME: Oldest pyramid in Egypt; earliest stone building in Egypt

The Step Pyramid at Saqqara

The 3rd Dynasty architect Imhotep built a tomb for King Djoser in the Saqqara cemetery in northern Egypt. At first Imhotep built his king a mastaba tomb—a square, boxlike tomb with an underground burial chamber. But then the plans were changed. Imhotep first converted the square tomb into a rectangular tomb, then into a four-stepped pyramid. Finally, it became a six-stepped pyramid. This was Egypt's first pyramid, and first stone building.

THE PYRAMID COMPLEX

The Step Pyramid is surrounded by a series of ceremonial buildings and courtyards, all protected by an enormous limestone wall. Archaeologists do not fully understand the significance of these buildings.

Stolen covering
The limestone covering was stolen in antiquity. No pyramid in Egypt today has been left with its covering intact.

Limestone casing
Originally the pyramid was covered in valuable, fine limestone, which made it sparkle in the strong Egyptian sunlight.

Underground maze
Underground passages surround the burial chamber.

Djoser's Step Pyramid

The six steps of the pyramid are obvious, but hidden beneath is King Djoser's burial chamber. It is surrounded by a maze of corridors, some of which are decorated with blue-green tiles and images of the king.

Stripped away *With the original fine limestone casing stripped from the pyramid, the building blocks beneath are exposed. This allows archaeologists to see the building stages of the pyramid.*

Four-stepped pyramid
Imhotep's original pyramid design of four steps is hidden within the larger six-stepped pyramid.

Unexplored area
The area to the north of the pyramid is still unexcavated. Many more rooms and tombs may lie beneath the rubble and sand.

Underground shaft
This shaft leads to the burial chamber beneath the pyramid.

Stepped corridor
Builders used this corridor to access the burial shaft.

Vertical shafts
Eleven vertical shafts lead to small burial passageways where the king's family may have been buried.

Burial chamber *Djoser's mummy was stolen many years ago, but archaeologists did find some human bones in his burial chamber.*

2649 BC
OLD KINGDOM
2150 BC
2040 BC
MIDDLE KINGDOM
1640 BC
1550 BC
NEW KINGDOM
1070 BC
712 BC
LATE PERIOD
332 BC

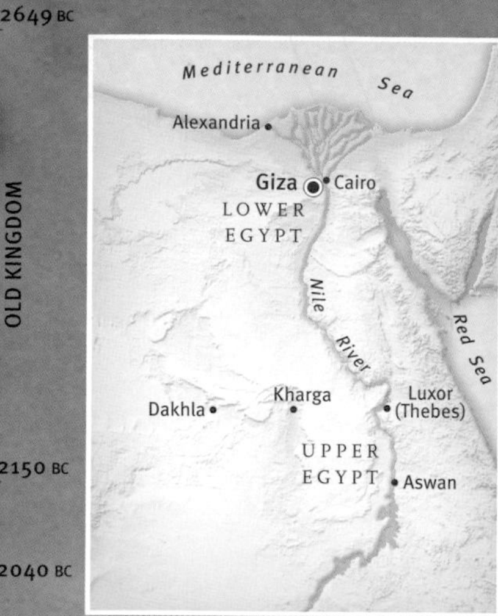

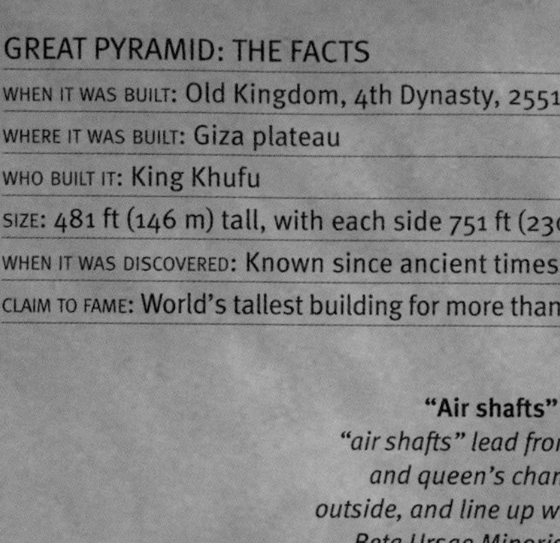

GREAT PYRAMID: THE FACTS

WHEN IT WAS BUILT:	Old Kingdom, 4th Dynasty, 2551–2528 BC
WHERE IT WAS BUILT:	Giza plateau
WHO BUILT IT:	King Khufu
SIZE:	481 ft (146 m) tall, with each side 751 ft (230 m) long
WHEN IT WAS DISCOVERED:	Known since ancient times
CLAIM TO FAME:	World's tallest building for more than 4,000 years

The Great Pyramid at Giza

Of the Seven Wonders of the Ancient World, the Great Pyramid of Giza is the only one that remains. A marvel of precision engineering, the pyramid was built as a tomb for the 4th Dynasty king Khufu. Although the central burial chamber still holds the king's sarcophagus, the pyramid was robbed in antiquity and the king's mummy has never been found.

King's chamber *The only completed burial chamber in the pyramid, the king's chamber now contains an empty sarcophagus.*

"Air shafts" *Two narrow "air shafts" lead from the king's and queen's chambers to the outside, and line up with the stars Beta Ursae Minoris and Sirius. They are unlikely to be practical air shafts, but probably had a ritual purpose.*

Queen's chamber *Early Arab visitors called this unfinished chamber of unknown ritual purpose the queen's chamber.*

Incredible size *These Egyptians are shown to scale with the Great Pyramid at Giza.*

Subterranean chamber *The purpose of this unfinished underground chamber is unknown.*

Millions of building blocks

It is estimated that there are as many as 2.3 million blocks in the pyramid, but this may well be an exaggeration—there could be lots of rubble in the solid parts of the pyramid. The stone came from a limestone quarry close by the pyramid site.

GUARDING THE ROYAL PYRAMIDS

Egyptian sphinxes were mythological beasts with a lion's body and a human, ram, or hawk head. The Egyptians believed that the Giza sphinx was a form of the sun god.

King Amasis in the form of a sphinx

The Great Sphinx
Built by King Khaefre, the Giza sphinx has a lion's body and the king's head. It wears a king's headcloth and once had a long beard.

Casing removed *The Great Pyramid was originally covered with an outer casing of fine limestone blocks. These were removed many years ago, and used to build parts of medieval Cairo.*

Almost perfect *The four sides of the pyramid exactly face north, south, east, and west. The base of the pyramid is an almost perfect square.*

Grand gallery *A sloping corridor lined with polished limestone leads to the king's chamber.*

Khaefre *Khaefre was Khufu's son. Khaefre's pyramid is smaller than the Great Pyramid, but looks larger because it was built on higher ground.*

Khufu *Khufu's Great Pyramid was surrounded by mastaba tombs built for the wealthy elite, and three queen's pyramids. Originally there was a mortuary temple attached to the pyramid, but this has vanished.*

Menkaure *The grandson of Khufu, Menkaure, built one large pyramid, plus three smaller pyramids for the most important royal women.*

2649 BC

OLD KINGDOM

2150 BC

2040 BC

MIDDLE KINGDOM

1640 BC

1550 BC

NEW KINGDOM

1070 BC

712 BC

LATE PERIOD

332 BC

Valley of the Kings

The kings of the Old and Middle kingdoms employed many thousands of workers to build pyramids in northern Egypt. Unfortunately, their pyramids were robbed soon after their funerals. During the New Kingdom, kings were buried in southern Egypt. Here they started a new tradition. Royal tombs were split into two completely separate parts. Royal mortuary temples—temples dedicated to the cult of the dead king—were built close by the Nile where everyone could see them. But the royal mummies were buried, with a vast range of precious grave goods, in secret rock-cut tombs hidden in the Valley of the Kings. Unfortunately, this did not save them from the robbers.

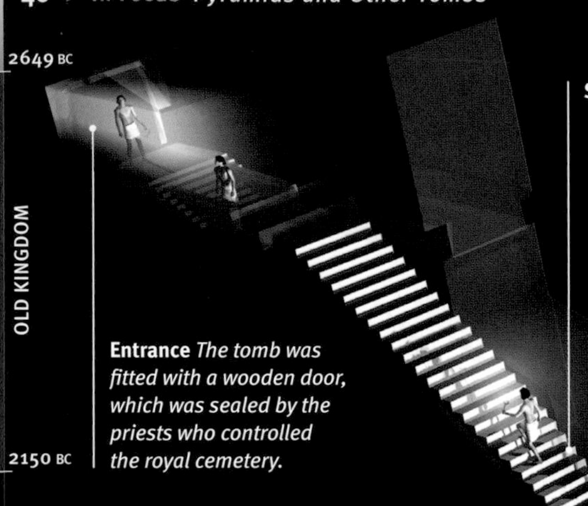

Entrance *The tomb was fitted with a wooden door, which was sealed by the priests who controlled the royal cemetery.*

Stairway

First passageway *Religious texts and scenes of the king standing with the sun god Re-Horakhty decorate these walls.*

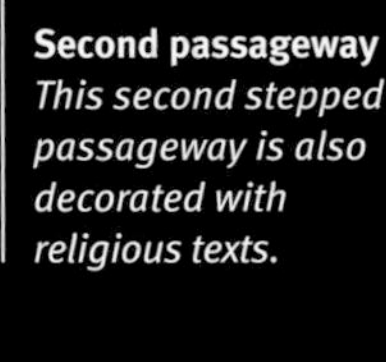

Second passageway *This second stepped passageway is also decorated with religious texts.*

Third passageway *Scenes from the Book of the Dead are illustrated here.*

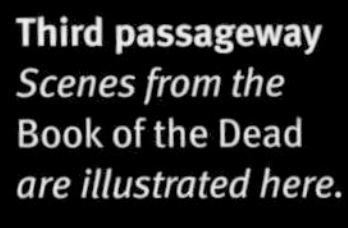

Well *The well was designed to protect the tomb from floodwater and from robbers!*

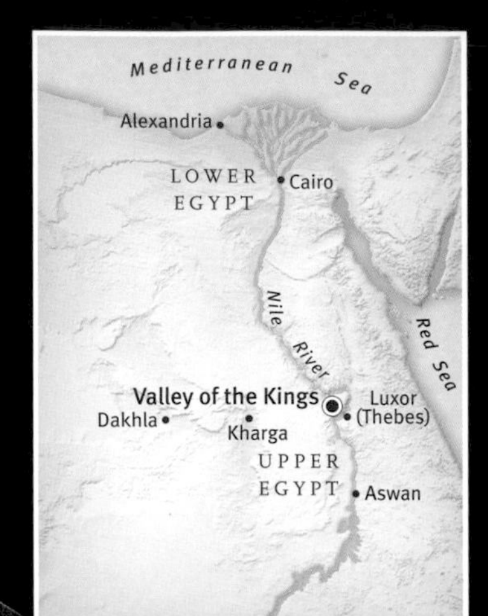

VALLEY OF THE KINGS: THE FACTS

WHEN IT WAS BUILT: New Kingdom, 18th–20th Dynasties, 1550–1070 BC

WHERE IT WAS BUILT: Western Thebes

WHO BUILT IT: Theban kings of the New Kingdom

SIZE: There are two clusters of royal tombs, one in the main valley, and one in the western valley (an offshoot). Put together, the two main areas come to significantly less than one square mile (2.6 sq km)

WHEN IT WAS DISCOVERED: Site was known since ancient times, but many tombs were discovered from 1817 to 1922

CLAIM TO FAME: Burial ground of many of the most famous kings, including Hatshepsut, Tuthmosis III, Tutankhamen, Seti I, and Ramesses II

Rock-cut tomb of Seti I

The tomb of the 19th Dynasty king Seti I was discovered in 1817 by Giovanni Battista Belzoni. It is the longest and deepest of the royal tombs, and one of the most wonderfully decorated.

The royal valley
The Valley of the Kings is a remote, dry river valley on the west bank of the Nile at Thebes, in southern Egypt. It was hoped that this remote location would protect the royal burials from tomb robbers who had emptied the royal pyramids.

Tomb raiders
Seti I's tomb was robbed in antiquity, but thieves left behind the king's beautiful calcite sarcophagus.
Antechamber *The antechamber is decorated with images of Seti I and the gods of ancient Egypt.*
Burial chamber *The ceiling of the burial chamber is decorated with images of gods and constellations, and with astronomical texts. This is where Seti I's mummy was placed.*
Lower passageway
Stairway *This unfinished stairway leads down into the bedrock. It has no known purpose.*
First pillared hall *Both the pillared hall and the pillared side room are decorated with religious texts.*

2649 BC
OLD KINGDOM
2150 BC
2040 BC
MIDDLE KINGDOM
1640 BC
1550 BC
NEW KINGDOM
1070 BC
712 BC
LATE PERIOD
332 BC

Mediterranean Sea
Alexandria
LOWER EGYPT
Cairo
Nile River
Red Sea
Valley of the Kings
Luxor (Thebes)
Dakhla
Kharga
UPPER EGYPT
Aswan

TUTANKHAMEN: THE FACTS

WHEN IT WAS BUILT: New Kingdom, 18th Dynasty, 1352–1346 BC

WHERE IT WAS BUILT: Valley of the Kings

WHO BUILT IT: A noble, but used by Tutankhamen who died suddenly

SIZE: Four chambers occupying 900 sq ft (84 sq m)

WHEN IT WAS DISCOVERED: 1922, by Howard Carter and Lord Carnarvon

CLAIM TO FAME: The most undisturbed tomb of a pharaoh to be discovered in modern times

The Tomb of Tutankhamen

Today Tutankhamen is the best known of all the Egyptian pharaohs, but he was a short-lived ruler. He came to the throne when he was only 8 years old and had died by the time he was 18 or 19 years old, possibly from a chariot accident. Tutankhamen's fame rests on the discovery of his tomb in 1922. Filled with magnificent treasures that were meant to help him in the afterlife, it was the only royal tomb that had not been seriously looted in ancient times. However, it had been robbed at least twice before its discovery by Howard Carter.

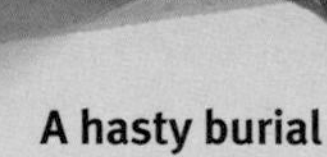

A hasty burial
Scientists have examined Tutankhamen's mummy but have not been able to find out what killed the pharaoh at such a young age. Because he died suddenly, a royal tomb was not ready and he was buried in a small tomb built for a noble.

Great determination
Funded by Lord Carnarvon, the English archaeologist Howard Carter spent 5 years searching for Tutankhamen's tomb, and another 10 years removing its treasures. He is shown here painstakingly cleaning the pharaoh's third coffin.

Precious sandals
The treasures found in the tomb included 47 pairs of thong sandals. The soles of some gilded pairs were decorated with images of the pharaoh's enemies.

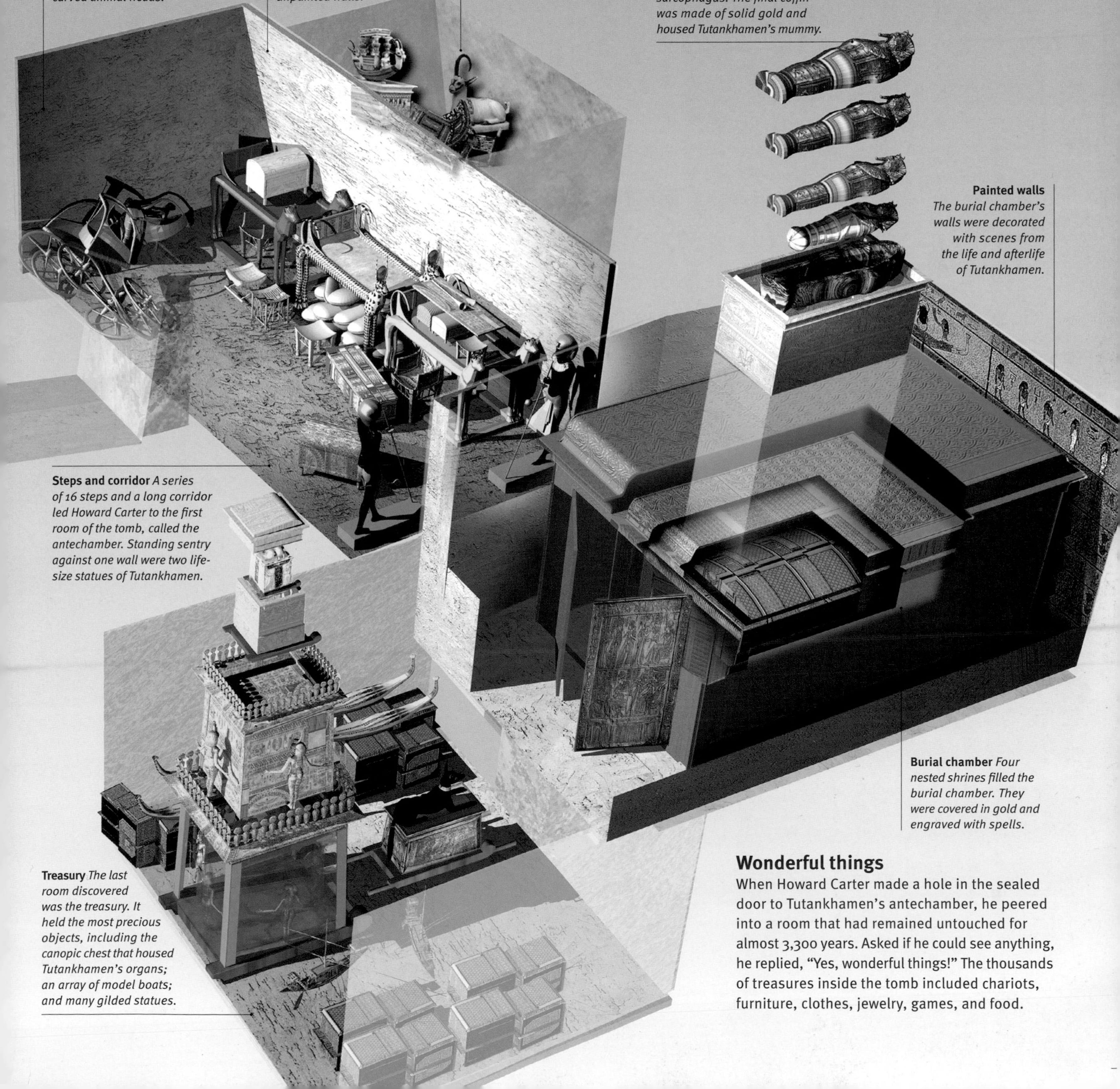

Antechamber *The antechamber was piled high with all manner of treasures. It was dominated by three gilded beds featuring carved animal heads.*

Unfinished tomb *The burial chamber was the only room in the tomb that was finished. The others still had rough, unpainted walls.*

Annex *Like the antechamber, the annex was crowded with objects, including low beds, chairs, and games.*

Nested coffins *It took Carter a year to remove the shrines and discover three beautiful nested coffins inside a stone sarcophagus. The final coffin was made of solid gold and housed Tutankhamen's mummy.*

Painted walls *The burial chamber's walls were decorated with scenes from the life and afterlife of Tutankhamen.*

Steps and corridor *A series of 16 steps and a long corridor led Howard Carter to the first room of the tomb, called the antechamber. Standing sentry against one wall were two life-size statues of Tutankhamen.*

Burial chamber *Four nested shrines filled the burial chamber. They were covered in gold and engraved with spells.*

Treasury *The last room discovered was the treasury. It held the most precious objects, including the canopic chest that housed Tutankhamen's organs; an array of model boats; and many gilded statues.*

Wonderful things

When Howard Carter made a hole in the sealed door to Tutankhamen's antechamber, he peered into a room that had remained untouched for almost 3,300 years. Asked if he could see anything, he replied, "Yes, wonderful things!" The thousands of treasures inside the tomb included chariots, furniture, clothes, jewelry, games, and food.

The Temple Complex of
Karnak

During the New Kingdom, the southern city of Thebes (modern Luxor) was Egypt's capital city. The most important collection of buildings in Thebes was the Karnak temple complex, a group of stone temples to the north of the city. The temples were dedicated to several gods, including the god of the empire, Amen; his wife, the goddess Mut; and their son, the god Khonsu.

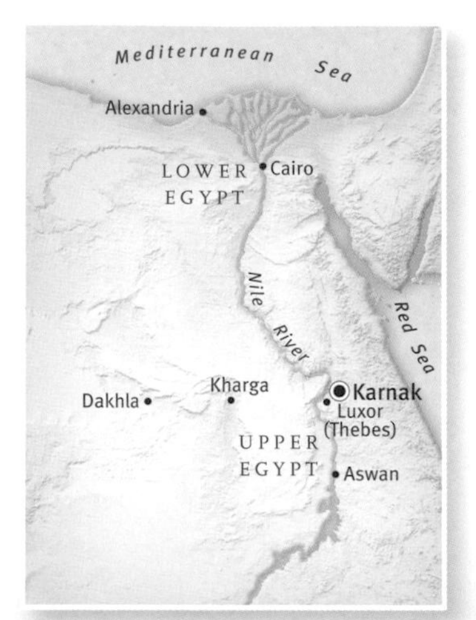

KARNAK: THE FACTS

WHEN IT WAS BUILT: From the Middle Kingdom until the Roman Period. Much of what is visible today was built from the early 18th Dynasty to the mid-19th Dynasty (c. 1550–1250 BC)

WHERE IT WAS BUILT: In the northern area of the ancient city of Thebes (modern Luxor)

WHO BUILT IT: Begun by Middle Kingdom kings but added to by many later rulers

SIZE: 5 acres (2 ha); 1 x 0.5 miles (1.6 x 0.8 km)

WHEN IT WAS DISCOVERED: Always known. The first visitors to Egypt thought it was a royal palace

CLAIM TO FAME: Largest of all remaining temples in Egypt

PROCESSIONAL WAY

Lines of ram-headed sphinxes guard the processional way running south from the Karnak Temple of Amen to the Luxor Temple. The statue of Amen was carried along this roadway when it was brought to Thebes.

Pylon One *The first temple gateway had flagpoles.*

Boat Shrine *This stand held the sacred boat of the god Amen. It was built by Seti II.*

Pylon Two

Barque Station *The Barque Station was a chapel built to house the sacred boat of Amen.*

Inside the temple complex

The temples were linked together by processional roadways. There was a large sacred pool; many pylons, or gateways; and several tall standing stones called obelisks. Most of the stone for this massive building program was brought to Thebes by boat from the riverside sandstone quarries of southern Egypt.

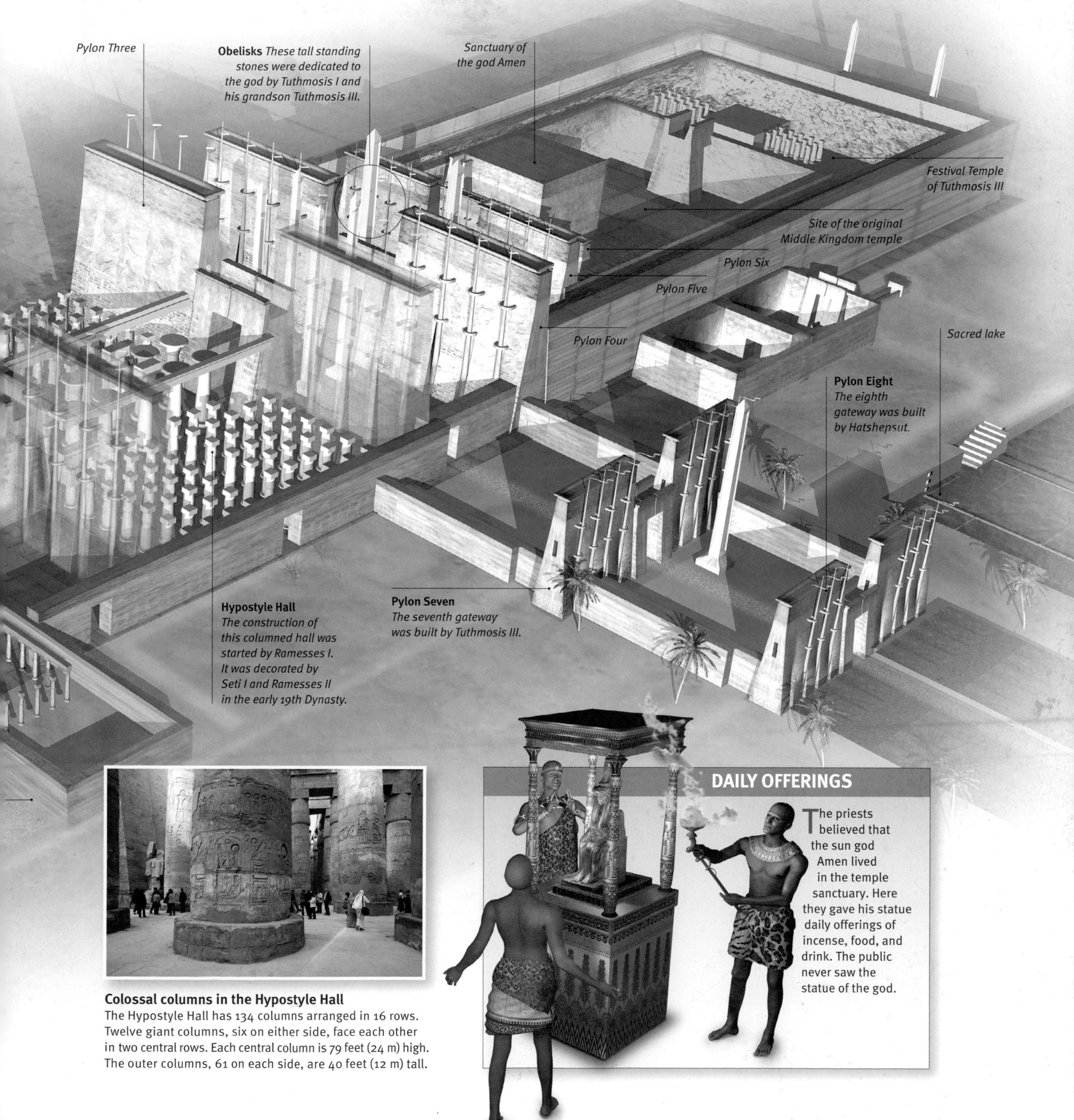

Colossal columns in the Hypostyle Hall
The Hypostyle Hall has 134 columns arranged in 16 rows. Twelve giant columns, six on either side, face each other in two central rows. Each central column is 79 feet (24 m) high. The outer columns, 61 on each side, are 40 feet (12 m) tall.

DAILY OFFERINGS

The priests believed that the sun god Amen lived in the temple sanctuary. Here they gave his statue daily offerings of incense, food, and drink. The public never saw the statue of the god.

2649 BC
OLD KINGDOM
2150 BC
2040 BC
MIDDLE KINGDOM
1640 BC
1550 BC
NEW KINGDOM
1070 BC
712 BC
LATE PERIOD
332 BC

The Tomb-workers' Village of

Deir el-Medina

The New Kingdom village of Deir el-Medina was built to house Egyptians who were working on the royal tombs in the Valley of the Kings and the nearby Valley of the Queens. The workmen lived in the village with their families and servants. But every week they left their houses and walked to the valleys. Here they stayed in temporary camps, returning to the village at the weekend. Deir el-Medina was built from stone and mud brick, and surrounded by a thick wall that stopped strangers from entering. The villagers, who were all skilled workmen, built their own impressive tombs outside the village wall.

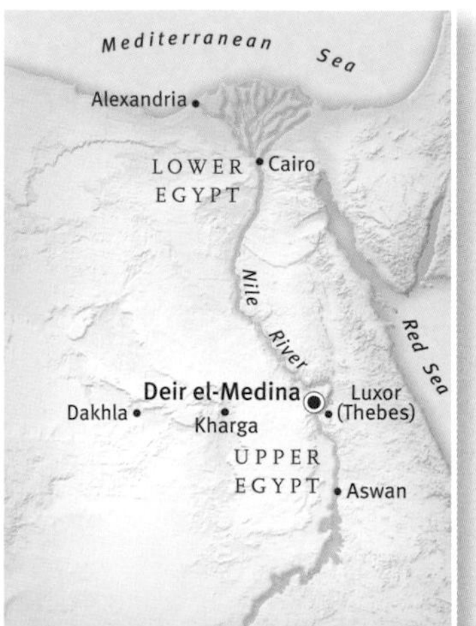

DEIR EL-MEDINA: THE FACTS

WHEN IT WAS BUILT: New Kingdom, 18th–20th Dynasties, 1550–1070 BC

WHERE IT WAS BUILT: Deir el-Medina, near Valley of the Kings in Western Thebes

WHO BUILT IT: Early New Kingdom pharaohs for workers building royal tombs

SIZE: Built as a walled village. There were 70 houses inside the village wall; tombs or tomb chapels outside the wall

WHEN IT WAS DISCOVERED: Excavated in 1920s by Bernard Bruyere

CLAIM TO FAME: Well-preserved New Kingdom tomb-workers' village

A house at Deir el-Medina

The terraced houses, all owned by the state, were long and dark. They must have been pleasantly cool in Egypt's hot summer months. Many of the villagers used the flat roofs as an extra room.

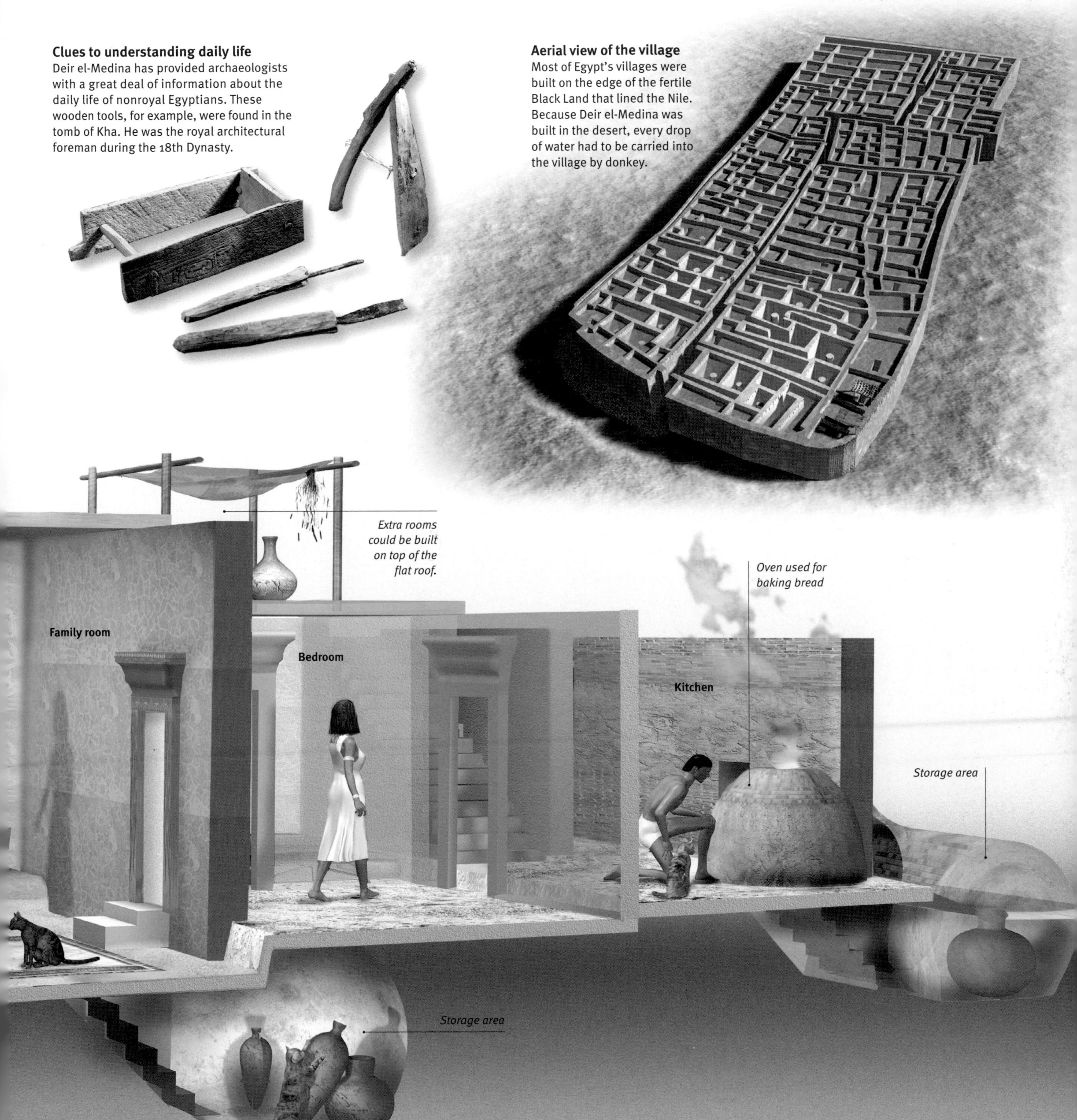

Clues to understanding daily life
Deir el-Medina has provided archaeologists with a great deal of information about the daily life of nonroyal Egyptians. These wooden tools, for example, were found in the tomb of Kha. He was the royal architectural foreman during the 18th Dynasty.

Aerial view of the village
Most of Egypt's villages were built on the edge of the fertile Black Land that lined the Nile. Because Deir el-Medina was built in the desert, every drop of water had to be carried into the village by donkey.

Mediterranean Sea
Alexandria
LOWER EGYPT
Cairo
Amarna
Nile River
Red Sea
Dakhla
Kharga
Luxor (Thebes)
UPPER EGYPT
Aswan

AMARNA: THE FACTS

WHEN IT WAS BUILT: New Kingdom, 18th Dynasty, 1348–1334 BC

WHERE IT WAS BUILT: Amarna, 194 miles (312 km) south of Cairo

WHO BUILT IT: King Akhenaten

SIZE: It is a large site, including the city, the separate workmen's village, and the royal tombs. The main city is about 6 miles (10 km) long x 1 mile (1.6 km) wide

WHEN IT WAS DISCOVERED: Known since antiquity; first serious survey in 1824. First excavation by Flinders Petrie in 1890s

CLAIM TO FAME: Short-lived capital of Egypt; escaped destruction because it was abandoned—probably during the second year of Tutankhamen's reign

The Aten
Akhenaten's god did not look like Egypt's other gods. It looked like the sun and had long, thin rays with miniature hands that held the *ankh*—the symbol of life.

City of the Heretic King

Amarna

In 1353 BC Amenhotep IV became king of Egypt. The new king did not worship the traditional gods. He had dedicated his life to just one god—a sun god known as The Aten. King Amenhotep changed his name to Akhenaten, which means "Living Spirit of The Aten." He abandoned the old capital city, Thebes, and started to build a new capital city that he called Akhetaten ("Horizon of The Aten"). Today this city is known as Amarna. It took just seven years to complete the new city, building with mud brick and stone. Akhenaten hoped that his city would last forever, but Amarna was abandoned after his death in 1335 BC.

Akhenaten's sun city

The new city included several royal palaces, two temples dedicated to The Aten, and the northern and southern suburbs, where Akhenaten's courtiers lived in spacious villas. A small workmen's village outside the main city housed the royal tomb-workers. The king and queen stood at the "Window of Appearance," on the bridge crossing the Royal Road, to greet their people below.

Storehouses of Ka, a life force created at birth and released at death

Palace storehouses

Royal Road *This processional way ran the length of the city.*

Great Temple to The Aten
This was an open-air temple, which allowed the priests to see the sun.

Palace gardens

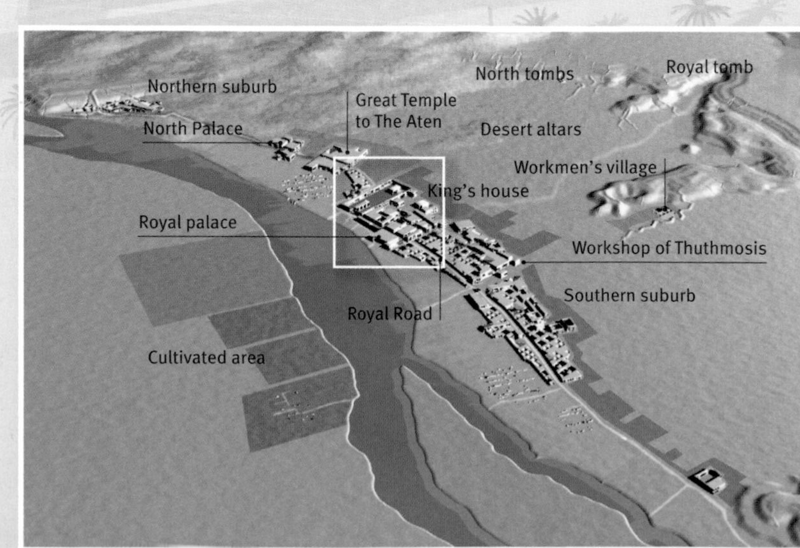

Map of Amarna
Amarna lies on the east bank of the Nile, halfway between the old capital cities of Thebes (south) and Memphis (north). Rock-cut tombs were cut into cliffs to the east of the city.

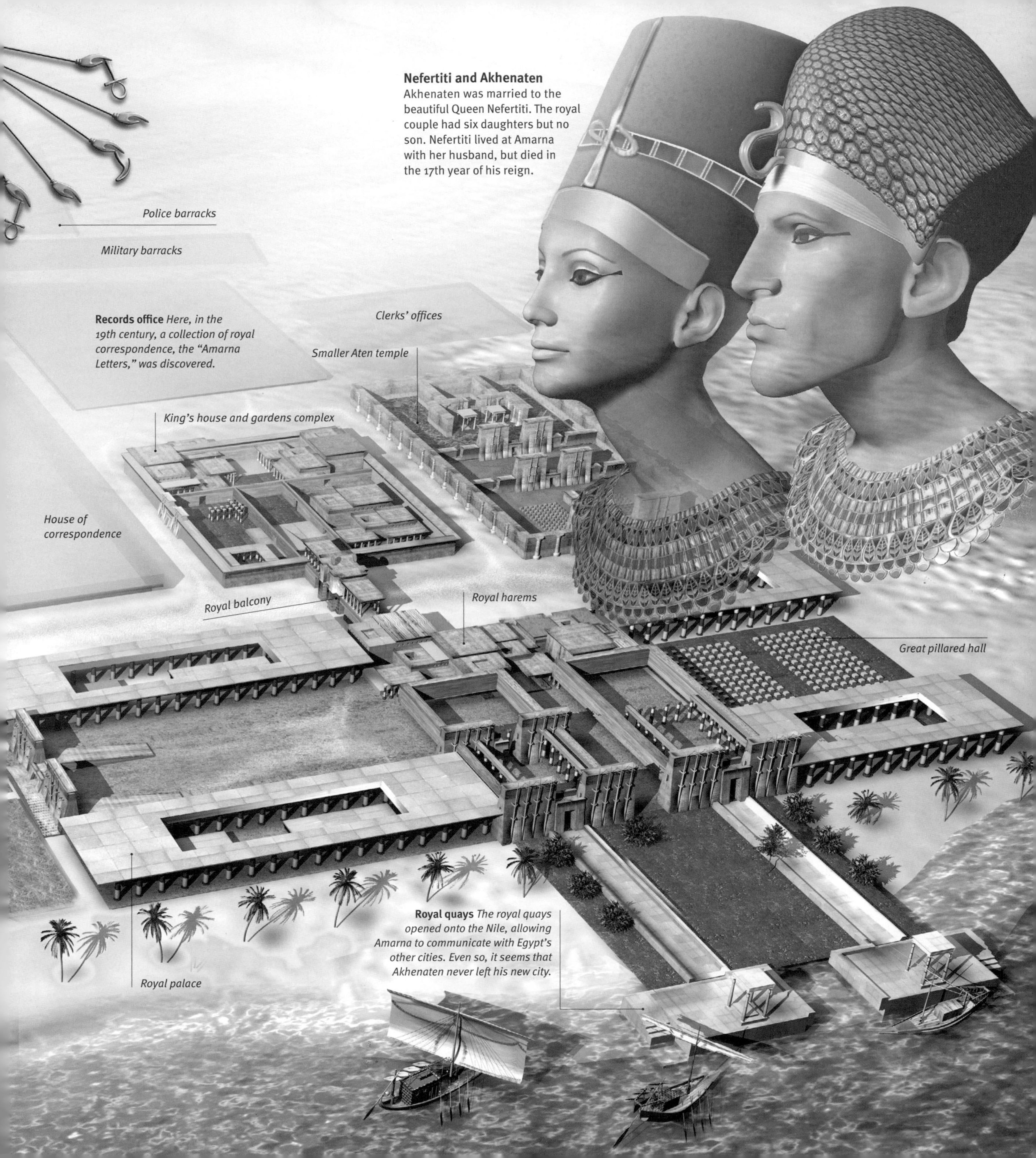

Nefertiti and Akhenaten
Akhenaten was married to the beautiful Queen Nefertiti. The royal couple had six daughters but no son. Nefertiti lived at Amarna with her husband, but died in the 17th year of his reign.
Police barracks
Military barracks
Records office *Here, in the 19th century, a collection of royal correspondence, the "Amarna Letters," was discovered.*
Clerks' offices
Smaller Aten temple
King's house and gardens complex
House of correspondence
Royal balcony
Royal harems
Great pillared hall
Royal quays *The royal quays opened onto the Nile, allowing Amarna to communicate with Egypt's other cities. Even so, it seems that Akhenaten never left his new city.*
Royal palace

The Fortress of Zawiyet umm El-Rakham

The large fortress-town of Zawiyet umm el-Rakham was founded by Ramesses II, known as "Ramesses the Great." The fortress was built to defend Egypt from Libyan tribesmen who were invading the fertile Nile Delta from the Western Desert. The fortress was protected by a thick mud-brick wall and had a heavily defended double gateway. Inside the fortress were barracks, a brewery, a bakery, a series of wells, and a temple. The governor's residence was an administrative center and also contained the private quarters of Troop Commander Neb-Re.

Zawiyet umm el-Rakham
Mediterranean Sea
Alexandria
LOWER EGYPT
Cairo
Nile River
Dakhla
Kharga
Luxor (Thebes)
UPPER EGYPT
Aswan

ZAWIYET UMM EL-RAKHAM: THE FACTS

WHEN IT WAS BUILT: New Kingdom, 19th Dynasty, about 1280 BC

WHERE IT WAS BUILT: Egypt's Mediterranean coast, 174 miles (280 km) west of Alexandria

WHO BUILT IT: King Ramesses II "The Great"

SIZE: More than 5 acres (2 ha)

WHEN IT WAS DISCOVERED: 1948; excavated since 1994 by Steven Snape, Liverpool University

CLAIM TO FAME: The largest surviving Egyptian fortress-town

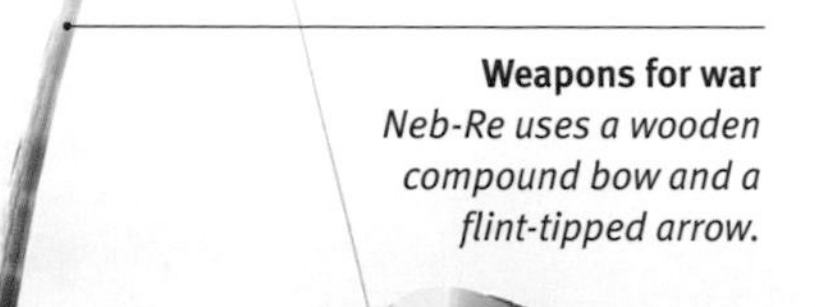

Weapons for war
Neb-Re uses a wooden compound bow and a flint-tipped arrow.

Ready for the fight
Neb-Re's chariot driver carries a shield to protect his master.

Protective blankets
Neb-Re's horses do not wear armor, but they both have protective blankets.

RECONSTRUCTING THE FORT

Seasonal rainfall has meant that today, little of the mud-brick fortress has survived above ground level. But through excavation, archaeologists have been able to reconstruct the groundplan (illustrated here). They estimate that the fortress held at least 500 soldiers. Some of the soldiers were probably accompanied by their families.

New Kingdom chariot
The chariot is light and easy to maneuver. Before the New Kingdom, chariots were not used by the Egyptian army.

Riding out in hot pursuit

Neb-Re, Troop Commander of Zawiyet umm el-Rakham, rides out from the fort in pursuit of Libyan tribesmen. Eventually, the Libyans forced the Egyptian troops to withdraw and the fortress was abandoned during the reign of King Merenptah, the son of Ramesses II.

The Great Temple at
Abu Simbel

Ramesses II built two rock-cut temples at Abu Simbel. The Smaller Temple was decorated with images of the king and his consort Nefertari, and was dedicated to the goddess Hathor. The Great Temple was decorated with four huge statues of the seated king. It was dedicated to four gods—Amen, Re-Horakhty, Ptah, and Ramesses himself. Abu Simbel was a remote place, far from any major town. Ramesses probably chose this site because the local geography allowed him to position his temple so that just twice each year, on the 20th of February and the 20th of October, the rising sun illuminated the statues of the four gods seated in the dark sanctuary.

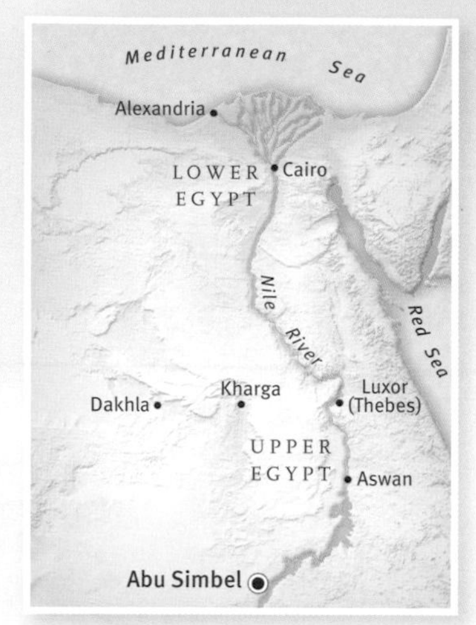

ABU SIMBEL: THE FACTS

WHEN IT WAS BUILT: During the reign of King Ramesses II, 19th Dynasty, 1290–1224 BC

WHERE IT WAS BUILT: Nubia

WHO BUILT IT: King Ramesses II

SIZE: Statues are each 65 ft (19.5 m) high. Façade is 98 ft (30 m) high and 115 ft (35 m) wide

WHEN IT WAS DISCOVERED: Always known by locals. Rediscovered, buried under sand, by Johann Ludwig Burckhardt in 1813

CLAIM TO FAME: Twin rock-cut tombs that were relocated during the 1960s

Inside the temple
The temple is cut 160 feet (48 m) into the sandstone of the Abu Simbel cliff. Inside there are pillared halls and a sanctuary.

Moving the temples

In the 1960s, the Aswan High Dam was built to provide Egypt with a controllable supply of water. Since the Abu Simbel temples lay below the new waterline, an international rescue mission was launched to lift the temples and part of the cliff face 215 feet (65 m) above their original site, safe from the rising waters of Lake Nasser.

Rescued from the water *The Smaller Temple is now secure in its new position within an artificial cliff.*

Expensive operation *The rescue operation took place between 1964 and 1968. It involved more than 1,700 workmen plus vast amounts of machinery. The temple relocations cost 36 million US dollars.*

New environment *The interior of the temple is housed in a concrete dome covered by an artificial hill.*

Final water level

One block at a time *The temple was cut into giant blocks. They were strengthened, then transported up the cliff face and reassembled.*

The original Great Temple *In its original position, the Great Temple was threatened by the waters of the artificial lake.*

Temple rescue *As work on the dam had already started, and the water level was rising, workers built a dam to protect the vulnerable sandstone from contact with the water.*

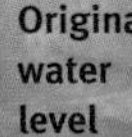

Original water level

To the sanctuary
Eight large statues line the temple entrance hall, four on each side. They show Ramesses II in the form of Osiris. The entrance hall leads to the temple sanctuary.

The Kings of Ancient Egypt

Prehistoric and Predynastic Period—before 3000 BC

In the predynastic period Egypt had many local kings ruling independent city-states, but no one king ruled the whole land until Narmer became Egypt's first king.

Early Dynastic Period 3000–2649 BC Dynasties 1–2

A confusing sequence of kings ruled a united Egypt from Memphis in this period. These early kings were buried either at Saqqara or Abydos.

Old Kingdom 2649–2150 BC Dynasties 3–6

3RD DYNASTY
Nebka I ?
Djoser
Sekhemkhet ?
Khaba
Sanakht
Huni

4TH DYNASTY
Snefru
Khufu
Djedefre
Khafre
Nebka II ?
Menkaure
Shepseskaf

5TH DYNASTY
Userkaf
Sahure
Neferirkare
Raneferef
Shepseskare ?
Neuserre
Menkauhor
Djedkare-Isesi
Unas

6TH DYNASTY
Teti
Userkare
Pepi I
Merenre I
Pepi II

First Intermediate Period 2150–2040 BC Dynasties 7–11

Egypt was no longer one united land. A confusing sequence of local kings ruled during the first intermediate period, until the Theban kings became strong enough to reunify Egypt and bring stability back to the kingdom.

Middle Kingdom 2040–1640 BC Dynasties 11–14

LATE 11TH DYNASTY
Mentuhotep II Nebhepetre
Mentuhotep III
Mentuhotep IV

12TH DYNASTY
Amenemhat I
Senwosret I
Amenemhat II
Senwosret II
Senwosret III
Amenemhat III
Amenemhat IV
Sobeknofru (female king)

13TH AND 14TH DYNASTIES
A confusing sequence of local kings

The Egyptian dynasties

For more than 3,000 years Egypt was ruled by kings, including some female kings. Historians divide these kings into dynasties—lines of kings who were usually, but not necessarily, blood relatives. The dating of the early kings of Egypt is not known with certainty. A question mark is placed next to the names of those kings for whom we have inconclusive records.

Second Intermediate Period 1640–1550 BC
Dynasties 15–17

The kingdom was divided in two during this period. Northern Egypt was ruled by the foreign "Hyksos" kings; southern Egypt was ruled from Thebes by local kings. Eventually the Theban kings grew strong enough to defeat the Hyksos and unite Egypt.

New Kingdom
1550–1070 BC
Dynasties 18–20

18TH DYNASTY
Ahmose
Amenhotep I
Tuthmosis I
Tuthmosis II
Tuthmosis III and
Hatshepsut (female king)
Tuthmosis III
Amenhotep II
Tuthmosis IV
Amenhotep III
Akhenaten (Amenhotep IV)
Smenkhkare
Tutankhamen
Aye
Horemheb

19TH DYNASTY
Ramesses I
Seti I
Ramesses II ("The Great")
Merenptah
Seti II
Amenmesse
Siptah
Tawosret (female king)

20TH DYNASTY
Sethnakhte
Ramesses III
Ramesses IV
Ramesses V
Ramesses VI
Ramesses VII
Ramesses VIII
Ramesses IX
Ramesses X
Ramesses XI

Third Intermediate Period 1070–712 BC
Dynasties 21–24

Again the Egyptian kindgom was divided in two. Egypt's kings ruled northern Egypt from the Nile Delta; the high priests of the god Amen controlled southern Egypt from Thebes. This led to a period of foreign rule.

Late Period
712–332 BC
Dynasties 25–31

25TH DYNASTY (NUBIAN RULERS)
Kashta
Piye
Shabaka
Shebitku
Taharqa
Tantamani

26TH DYNASTY
Necho I
Psamtek I
Necho II
Psamtek II
Apries
Amasis
Psamtek III

27TH DYNASTY (PERSIAN RULERS)
Cambyses II
Darius I
Xerxes I
Artaxerxes I
Xerxes II
Darius II
Artaxerxes II

28TH DYNASTY
Amyrtaios

29TH DYNASTY
Nefarud I
Pasherenmut
Hagar
Nefarud II

30TH DYNASTY
Nectanebo I
Djedhor
Nectanebo II

31ST DYNASTY (PERSIAN RULERS)
Artaxerxes III
Arses
Darius III

Ptolemaic Period
332–30 BC

MACEDONIAN DYNASTY (332–302 BC)
Alexander III ("The Great")
Philip III Arrhidaeus
Alexander IV

PTOLEMAIC PERIOD
Ptolemy I Soter I
Ptolemy II Philadelphus
Ptoelmy III Euergetes I
Ptolemy IV Philopator
Ptolemy V Epiphanes
Ptolemy VI Philometor
Ptolemy VI Philometor and
Ptolemy VIII Euergetes II
Ptolemy VI Philometor
Ptolemy VIII Euergetes II
Ptolemy IX Soter II
Ptolemy X Alexander I
Ptolemy IX Soter II
Ptolemy XI Alexander II and
Berenice III
Ptolemy XII Neos Dionysos
Berenice IV and Cleopatra VI
Ptolemy XII Neos Dionysos
Cleopatra VII and Ptolemy XIII
Cleopatra VII and Ptolemy XIV
Cleopatra VII and
Ptolemy XV Caesar

Roman conquest 30 BC

Glossary

AD An abbreviation for the Latin "anno Domini," meaning "in the year of our Lord." Used for the measurement of time, AD indicates the number of years since the supposed date of Christ's birth.

afterlife The life that the ancient Egyptians hoped to live after death.

Akhet The season of flooding or inundation. The yearly flooding of the Nile valley occurred from July to October.

Amen The most important state god of New Kingdom Egypt. Amen's main temple was at Karnak (ancient Thebes; modern Luxor).

Amen-Re A fusion of the gods Amen and Re.

amulet A charm or piece of jewelry worn as protection against evil.

ankh A symbol that meant life. It was carried by gods, kings, and queens.

antechamber An outer room leading to a main room or chamber, often found in pyramids and rock-cut tombs.

Anubis Jackal-headed god of cemeteries and mummification who presided over the "weighing of the heart ceremony."

archaeologist A person who excavates and studies the material remains of the human past.

Aswan High Dam A dam built in the 1960s to allow the Egyptians to control the waters of the Nile. The temples at Abu Simbel were moved to higher ground due to the flooding of this area.

Aten *See* The Aten.

Atum A god of creation.

BC An abbreviation for "before Christ." Used for the measurement of time, BC indicates the number of years before the supposed date of Christ's birth.

Black Land The fertile land in the Nile valley and Delta. The Egyptians called this land "kemet."

Book of the Dead A papyrus paper scroll covered with magical texts and pictures. A copy of the *Book of the Dead* was placed in the tomb with the deceased person to help him or her pass through the dangers of the underworld.

burial chamber The main room in a pyramid or rock-cut tomb, where the body was placed.

canopic jars Jars for storing the stomach, lungs, intestines, and liver of a mummified body.

cartouche An oval shape drawn around the hieroglyphic name of a king or queen of Egypt.

civilization An organized society that has developed social customs, government, technology, and arts.

crook A stick with a curved top carried by a god or pharaoh to symbolize kingship.

Delta The fertile area to the north of modern Cairo, where the Nile branches before emptying into the Mediterranean Sea. The Delta is often called Lower, or Northern, Egypt.

demotic script A form of writing that developed from the hieratic script in approximately 700 BC. It was used for administration and business.

Dynastic Age The time, from about 3000 BC to 30 BC, when Egypt was ruled by dynasties of kings.

dynasty A line of ruling kings who often, but not always, belonged to one family. Thirty-one numbered dynasties plus the Macedonian and Ptolemaic kings ruled ancient Egypt.

Egyptologist A specialist archaeologist who finds out about how people lived in ancient Egypt by studying their writings and their material remains.

embalmer A person who treats a dead body with spices and oils to prevent it from decaying.

faience A glasslike material used for making cups, jars, and amulets. It was made by heating up powdered quartz in a mold.

flail A whip carried by a god or king.

flax A plant whose stalks can be spun and woven into linen cloth.

frieze A strip of painting or carving on a temple or a tomb wall that tells a story.

gild To cover in gold leaf.

gold leaf A very thin sheet of beaten gold.

Hathor The goddess of motherhood, music, and drunkenness. She sometimes takes the form of a beautiful woman, and sometimes takes the form of a cow.

hieratic script A faster form of writing than hieroglyphs. It was always written from right to left, unlike hieroglyphics, which could be written in any direction.

hieroglyphs The symbols and pictures of ancient Egyptian writing.

Hittites Egypt's enemy during the reign of Ramesses II. The Hittite empire was based in modern Turkey.

Horus The son of Isis and Osiris. The living king of Egypt was linked to Horus, while his dead father was linked with the god Osiris.

Imhotep The 3rd Dynasty architect who designed the Step Pyramid for King Djoser.

incense An aromatic substance extracted from resin. Incense was burned in ritual ceremonies.

intermediate periods Times when Egypt was not one united land ruled by one king.

irrigate To water the land.

Isis A goddess, the wife of Osiris and mother of Horus. Isis was a powerful healer and magician.

Khonsu A god, the son of Amen and Mut.

Lower Egypt Northern Egypt; the Delta region north of modern Cairo.

market garden A garden used to grow fruit and vegetables for sale.

mastaba A rectangular stone or mud-brick tomb. Egypt's first kings were buried in mastabas.

mud brick A brick made from mud. Egypt's houses and palaces were built using sun-dried mud bricks made from thick Nile mud.

mummification A process of drying and bandaging that preserves the dead body of a person or an animal.

Mut A goddess, the wife of Amen.

natron A natural salt from the desert that absorbs moisture. The ancient Egyptians used natron to dry out bodies during mummification.

Nubia The land beyond Egypt's southern border at Aswan. Egypt's traditional enemy, and a valuable source of gold, Nubia was often included in the Egyptian Empire.

oasis (singular), **oases** (plural) A fertile region in the desert with its own water supply.

obelisk Tall, narrow, pointed standing stone.

"opening of the mouth ceremony" A ceremony performed by a priest during a funeral, which will help the soul of the dead person to come back to life.

Osiris God of the dead, also called the god-king of the afterlife, and Egypt's first mummy. Osiris was the husband of Isis and the father of Horus.

papyrus A plant that the ancient Egyptians used to make a form of paper, and to make boats.

pectoral A jeweled plaque worn as a pendant.

Peret A time of "coming forth." A season of four months from November to February when the farmers grew their crops.

pharaoh The king of ancient Egypt. The name comes from the ancient Egyptian word *per-ao*, meaning "the great house." It referred to the palace where the pharaoh lived.

pigment A colored powder that is mixed with a liquid to make ink or paint.

Ptah A god. Ptah's main temple was at Memphis, in Northern Egypt.

pylon A gateway to a fortress, palace, or temple between two large towers.

Re A sun god, the most important state god of Old Kingdom Egypt. Re's main temple was at Heliopolis (modern Cairo).

Red Land The desert that lay beyond the Black Land, the river valley, and the Delta. The ancient Egyptians called this land "deshret." Tombs and pyramids were built in the Red Land.

Re-Horakhty A sun god, a fusion of Re and Horus.

relief A carving on a stone surface.

ritual The procedure for a religious ceremony such as the "opening of the mouth."

Rosetta stone An inscribed slab of granite that gave the major clue to deciphering hieroglyphs, found in 1799. The stone is 3 ft 7 in (114 cm) high, 2 ft 3 in (72 cm) wide, and 11 in (28 cm) thick. It weighs 1,684 pounds (762 kg). The Rosetta stone is now in London's British Museum.

sarcophagus (singular), **sarcophagi** (plural) A large stone or wooden box that enclosed a mummy's coffin. The surfaces were often painted or carved in relief.

scribe A person, almost always a man, who could read and write.

Sekhmet A goddess who sometimes takes the form of a beautiful woman, and sometimes takes the form of a cat.

senet An Egyptian game played with a board and counters. It had lucky and unlucky squares and was a little like the modern game of backgammon.

Seth A mischievous god with a curious animal head. Seth is the brother of Isis and Osiris.

shabti A model figure that acted as the servant of the deceased and carried out all the work required in the afterlife.

shaduf An irrigation device made from a bucket and a counterweight. It was used to lift water from the Nile or from a canal to water gardens.

Shemu Egyptian summer, a season of three months from April to June.

sphinx A mythological beast with a human, ram, or bird head and the body of a lion.

temple sanctuary The innermost, most private part of the temple, where it was believed the temple god lived.

The Aten The god worshipped by the 18th Dynasty king Akhenaten. The Aten looked like a sun disk. The city of Amarna (ancient Akhetaten) was built to honor The Aten.

Thebes A southern city; the capital of Egypt during the New Kingdom. Now known as Luxor.

Thoth The scribe of the gods. Sometimes Thoth is shown as an ibis (a bird); at other times he takes the form of a baboon.

Upper Egypt Southern Egypt; the region south of modern Cairo.

uraeus The royal cobra worn on the forehead on crowns and royal headdresses.

vizier Chief adviser to the king and second only to him in importance. During the New Kingdom there were two viziers, one for Upper Egypt and one for Lower Egypt.

Index

Credits

The publisher thanks Alexandra Cooper and Steven Snape for their contributions, and Puddingburn for the index.

COVER AND ILLUSTRATIONS
Malcolm Godwin/Moonrunner Design

MAPS
Map Illustrations

PHOTOGRAPHS
l=left, r=right, tl=top left, tcl=top center left, tc=top center, tcr=top center right, tr=top right, cl=center left, c=center, cr=center right, b=bottom, bl=bottom left, bcl=bottom center left, bc=bottom center, bcr=bottom center right, br=bottom right

APL=Australian Picture Library; APL/CBT=Australian Picture Library/Corbis; BM=British Museum; GI=Getty Images; WF=Werner Forman Archive

8bl Australian Associated Press; **10**bcl, bcr, bl, tc WF; bl, tc, tl Steven Snape; br, c, cr, tr APL; cl BM; tr APL/CBT; **11**bcl, l, tr APL; bcr BM; br Corel Corp; br, cl, cr, tcl, tl, tr Steven Snape; br WF; cr Photodisc; tcl APL/CBT; tcr GI; tl PhotoEssentials; **13**cr Jurgen Liepe; **14**tr GI; **15**tc University of Dundee; tl GI; **16**br GI; cl, cr APL; **18**br WF; cl APL/CBT; **23**b, bl BM; bc, bcr APL; br APL/CBT; **24**cl BM; **27**tr GI; **30**br APL; **32**tr APL/CBT; **35**bcr BM; br, tr APL; **36**bcr APL; bl, tr APL/CBT; br, cl GI; **37**bcr, tr APL; c GI; **38**cl APL; **45**tcl APL; tr GI; **46**br GI; **48**bl, br WF; **51**bl APL/CBT; **53**tl APL/CBT

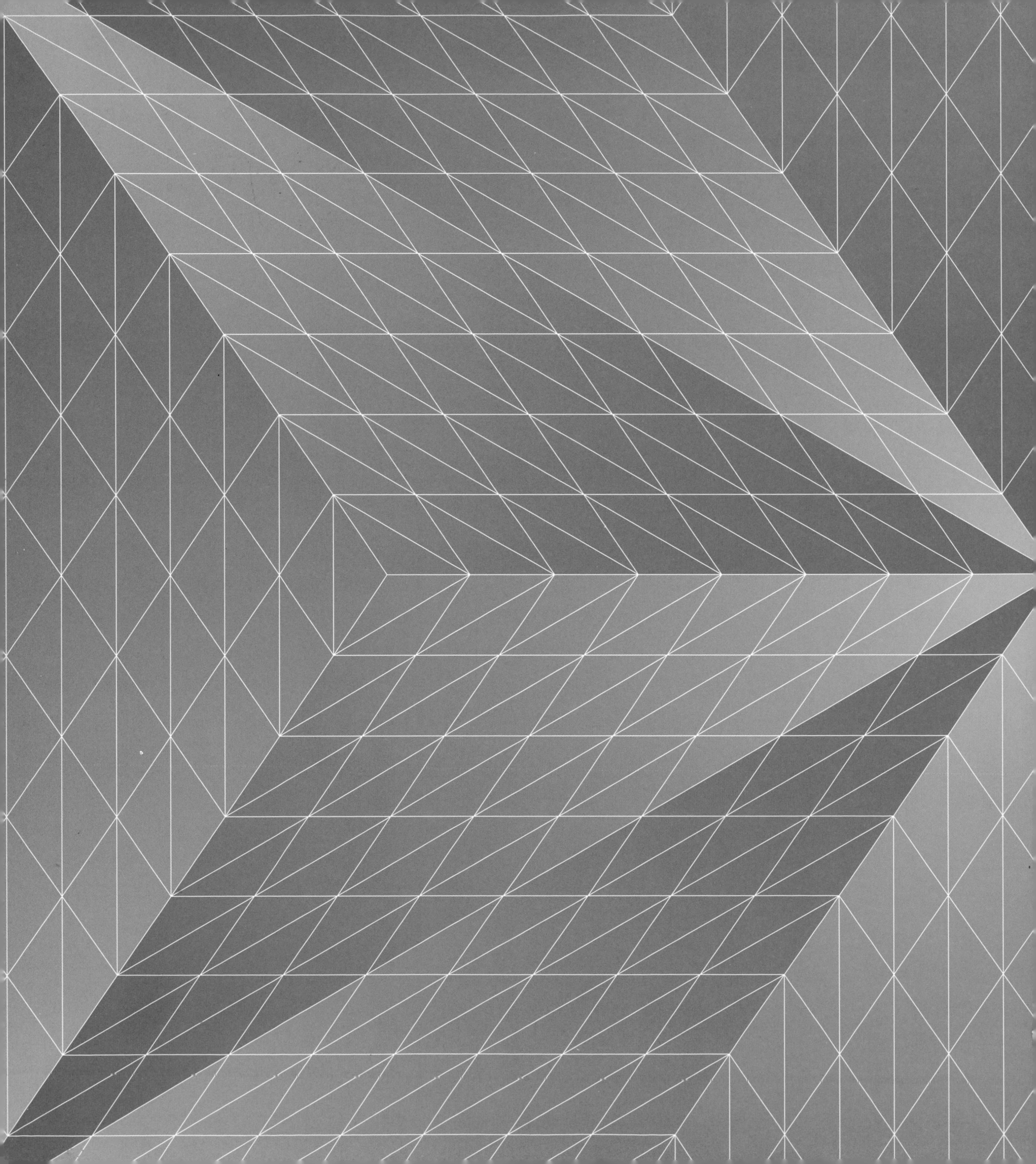